M₀...™

H₀... ...l Your

A... ...SHOP

DAVID H. JACOBS, JR.

D1471412

First published in 1993 by MBI Publishing Company, PO Box 1, 729 Prospect Avenue, Osceola, WI 54020-0001 USA

MBI Publishing Company books are also available at discounts in bulk quantity for industrial or sales-promotional use. For details write to Special Sales Manager at Motorbooks International Wholesalers & Distributors, 729 Prospect Avenue, PO Box 1, Osceola, WI 54020-0001 USA.

Library of Congress Cataloging-in-Publication Data
Jacobs, David H.
How to design and build your auto workshop /
David H. Jacobs, Jr.
p. cm. — (MBI Publishing Company PowerTech series)
Includes index.
ISBN 0-7603-0553-6
1. Automobile repair shops. 2. Workshops. I. Title.
II. Series.
TL153.J2597 1998
629.28'7—dc21   98-6437

On the front cover: In for tune-ups are a 1967 Ferrari 275 GTB / 4 and a 1997 Viper GTS coupe. Owner of these cars and the workshop in which they are parked is Michael McCafferty of Borrego Springs, California. *David Newhardt*

On the back cover: Top—A comfortable workshop environment wouldn't be complete without some "essential" extras. Note the stereo atop the cabinet and the poster and decals on its front. *Randy Johnson*. Bottom—Before purchasing garage doors, seriously consider what types of vehicles will be going in and out of your shop. Regular household garage doors like the one pictured are usually about 8 feet wide by 7 feet high.

Printed and bound in the United States of America

CONTENTS

ACKNOWLEDGMENTS

Automotive workshops in general may have similar basic designs and equipment setups, but each is unique according to the needs of its owner. In order to amass enough information to fill this book with numerous design and setup variations, many automotive professionals and avid car enthusiasts were contacted and interviewed. Likewise, technical help was received from building contractors, municipal building department officials, tool and equipment company executives, and others. I would like to thank all of them for their time, assistance, and enthusiastic support.

Makita USA, Inc., is a most appreciated supporter. Through the personal efforts and assistance of Roy Thompson, Makita's Product Marketing Manager, all of the construction power tools and equipment needed to construct a workshop were made available. These Makita products operated as advertised, easily and with controlled precision. The battery-operated tools were especially surprising, in that they had as much power and torque as many of their electrically driven counterparts. Their battery charges lasted a great deal longer than expected, too. I want to extend a special word of appreciation to Mr. Thompson and the entire Makita USA Corporation for their enthusiastic support and genuine consideration.

Jim Poluch and Christine Collins, advertising executives for The Eastwood Company, provided photos and samples from Eastwood's huge selection of automotive repair, restoration, and maintenance tools, equipment, and products. I want to thank them very much for their time and continued support. The Eastwood Company's tools and equipment are proven performers that help make automotive repair projects progress at faster rates, with accuracy and convenience.

The Stanley Works supplied hand tools and related accessories used to construct various building projects for this book. I must thank Francis Hummel, Director of Marketing for The Stanley Works, for his delightful interest and eager support.

Jim Yocum is a professional building contractor with years of experience hiding nails. I appreciate the time he and his partner, Jim Woodcock, spent with me to explain various construction methods and techniques.

I would also like to thank Carter and Pam Hoffmann for making their new garage/auto workshop available for photos, and Bob Greer and Matt Jacobs for their help during some photo sessions. I am also grateful for the ingenious Sta-Put Color Pegs provided by Jim Richeson, and the computer program entitled *The Home Series* provided by Suri Reddy, Associate Product Manager for Autodesk Retail Products. The program was used to produce line drawing illustrations featured in various chapters.

Gathering useful information about various automotive workshop designs and setups required input from a number of experienced auto professionals and serious enthusiasts. Hearty appreciation is extended to the following people for all of their information, time, patience, and opinions during interviews and through the mail, as well as for the permission to photograph their auto workplaces or other items of interest: Dan Mycon, owner of Newlook Autobody in Kirkland, Washington, and his chief auto body expert, Bill Snyder; Rick and Ron Weglin, owners of Harrah's Automotive in Seattle, Washington; Mike Putnam, manager of Mathewson's Automotive & Tire in Renton, Washington; Garry Allen, owner of Jags Plus, Inc., in Everett, Washington; Mike Holiman, chief sprint car mechanic from Marysville, Washington; editor Bill Cannon and contributors to *Skinned Knuckles Magazine* in Monrovia, California; Colley Matheny, manager of Wesco Autobody Supply in Kirkland, Washington; John Roberts from Bothell, Washington, avid restorer of 1955-1957 Chevrolets; Jack Holden, owner of Champion Import Service in Kirkland, Washington; Steve Johnson, manager of the Minit-Lube facility in Kirkland, Washington; the folks at Thurman Electric & Plumbing Supply in Kirkland, Washington; John Lemm of Alki Lumber in Seattle, Washington; Roy Dunn, owner of Auto Accents in Des Moines, Washington; Joe Christensen and Don Knowland of the Smithy Company in The Dalles,

Oregon; and Nettie Gilruth of Mercer Island, Washington.

In addition to those just mentioned, I want to thank the following individuals and the companies they represent for supplying photos or products used in photo sessions and other related activities: Terry Ehrich of Hemmings Motor News; Hilarie Meyer, Campbell Hausfeld; Rob Guzikowski, Simpson Strong-Tie; Jeff Tennant of Exhaust-Away; Stan Erwine, American Tool Companies, Inc.; David Martel, Harbor Freight Tools; Helsper Sewing Products; Michael Brainerd of Dremel; Jeff Noland, HTP America, Inc.; John Pfanstiehl, Pro Motorcar Products, Inc.; Jeff Gaul, MSD Ignition; Bill Cork, Plano Molding Company; Fred LoBianco, California Car Cover Company; D. R. Zivko, Wickliffe Industries, Inc.; Pat Parker, Cover-It Instant Garages; Gary Busha, Snap-on Tools Corporation; Linda Toncray, PPG Industries, Inc.; Sally Anderson, The Chamberlain Group; Ron Ballard, Vermont American; and John Schoepke of Pine Ridge Enterprise.

As they have done many times before, Van and Kim Nordquist, owners of Photographic Designs in Mukilteo, Washington, did an outstanding job of developing film and turning hundreds of negatives into top-quality prints. I appreciate their attention to detail and their extra efforts in making sure each picture turned out perfect. I am also most grateful for the continued support, general assistance, and computer graphics provided by Janna Jacobs.

Finally, I wish to thank the professional staff of Motorbooks International. I am most grateful for the editorial assistance and overall enthusiasm generated by Tim Parker, Michael Dregni, Barbara Harold, Greg Field, Mike Dapper, Zack Miller, Mary LaBarre, and free lance copy editor Heather Aronson.

INTRODUCTION

In a most general sense, home-based automotive workshops are places where cars and trucks are tuned, repaired, restored, or generally cared for by enthusiastic, do-it-yourself automobile owners. Repair garages, on the other hand, are most commonly regarded as places where customers pay professional technicians good sums of money to make their private vehicles look or run like new. Although many of the operations undertaken in both facilities are quite similar, there is a profound difference between them.

Most car and truck owners associate professional repair garages with hard-earned money that must be spent on vehicles that break down at inopportune times. Conversely, avid do-it-yourselfers almost unanimously regard their personal auto workshops as havens where they can escape the hustle and bustle of everyday life to tinker, putter, fix, mend, caress, massage, restore, clean, detail, or admire their favorite motorized vehicles. These are places where auto enthusiasts eagerly turn rust buckets into dependable daily drivers, old sleds into show cars, and ordinary 4x4s into high-powered puddle jumpers.

Along with being set up to serve as practical and versatile repair centers, home workshops can also be outfitted with a number of creature comforts to make the time spent there more enjoyable. Many home shops are equipped with sound systems, televisions, refrigerators, microwave ovens, and bathrooms with large sinks. And why not? After all, working on cars is dirty work, and who wants grease-covered family members traipsing through their house in search of a quick peek at the television evening news, a cold drink, a hot snack, or an open door to the porcelain facility?

Just about everyone who enjoys spending time under the hood or chassis of a car or truck has visions of his or her own perfect workshop. John Pfanstiehl, owner of Pro Motorcar Products, Inc., in Clearwater, Florida, says his dream shop would have a twenty-four hour auto parts store/machine shop combination on one side, a huge, 'round-the-clock auto salvage yard on the other, and a full-service deli across the street with an aerobics gym on the second floor. Surely a workshop located amongst such a fine blend of advantageous services would be an ideal, if rather unrealistic, situation.

To compensate for a lack of such convenient and extraordinary workshop site features, you could simply design your own workplace to accommodate many of those needs. You could construct a full two-story workshop and take advantage of open space on the second floor for the storage of new auto parts and those hard-to-find relics you miraculously spot at swap meets and auctions. Or you might erect a two-story building with half of the top floor enclosed for storage and the other half open for tall vehicles that may need to be parked and/or worked on in that expansive space. A basement under your workshop can serve as an ideal storage area. To satisfy needs of a more personal nature, small refrigerators could be fit under bathroom counters, and little microwave ovens might be installed almost anywhere.

As far as workshop size is concerned, big is rarely big enough. Anyone designing an automotive workshop building should take into account that he or she may eventually want to expand it. Draw plans in such a way that an attractive and complimentary addition could be attached with minimal structural, electrical, or plumbing complications.

Auto enthusiasts enjoy wide ranges of various automotive upkeep, repair, and restoration endeavors. While some may prefer to concentrate on maximizing engine and drive train performance, others might strictly gear their activities toward body and paint specialities. Each area of automotive care requires different workshop designs and setups. One will need hoists, lifts, and stands for engines and transmissions where another will require floor anchors, wall-mounted lights, and a larger air compressor to supply any number of pneumatic sanders, grinders, sandblasters, and spray paint guns.

To be sure, there are basic principles to keep in mind for all automotive workshops regardless of their intended functions. Floors must be solid enough to withstand the weight of cars and pickup trucks; ceilings must be properly reinforced before hoists are bolted to them; roofs have to be properly shingled to prevent leaks; walls must be insulated to keep out winter cold and summer heat; workbenches should be built with sturdy materials and strong joints to support heavy auto parts and assemblies; and all electrical panels, wires, switches, outlets, and junction boxes must be installed according to building code standards and specifications.

Personal safety should be everyone's primary concern. This issue must never be overlooked or underestimated. Respirators, goggles, full face shields, welder's aprons, gloves, and safety shoes are indispensable. Their use will go a long way toward preserving your health and preventing unnecessary injuries. Equally important are fire extinguishers and fully equipped first aid kits. Hopefully, you will never need a fire extinguisher or first aid kit, but if or when you do, nothing could possibly replace them. A shop telephone is also regarded as a safety item and should be located close to an outside door (away from potential hazards more commonly found near a shop's center).

This book examines many automotive workshop ideas from both professional automobile technicians and avid, experienced auto enthusiasts. While their suggestions or shop features may not always coincide with your needs or desires, they come from people who are active in the auto repair/restoration fields with years of experience behind them. Except for safety concerns, which can almost always be enhanced, the features described in this book are intended as guides for those who have finally found a way to build their own dream workshops. Whether you plan to build a separate auto workshop facility or remodel an existing home garage into a viable workshop space, I hope this book gives you many useful tips for designing an automotive workshop that meets all of your needs and expectations.

CHAPTER 1

BASIC IDEAS

Automobile enthusiasts are generally regarded as people who enjoy maintaining and repairing automobiles no matter where these tasks must be accomplished. Although many auto aficionados have fond memories of parking outdoors, lifting meager tool boxes from car trunks, and tackling maintenance tasks that ranged from simple oil changes to full tune-ups, there is no doubt that a first-class workshop is nearly always preferable to the great outdoors.

Crude working conditions may make for amusing memories, but as time passes a "mobile repair facility" quickly becomes more of a hassle than an adventure. People active in the automotive field quickly amass large assortments of tools and other auto-related equipment. In the blink of an eye, it seems, trunks are soon too small to carry these items, and storage becomes a primary concern. This is when most enthusiasts start realistically pondering their tool and equipment storage and automotive workshop options.

Many of the most desired features of an ideal automotive workshop are depicted here. Along with a two-post lift, note the engine exhaust ventilation tubing and ducting, a wall-mounted telephone next to a first floor parts storage area, an upstairs office with restroom, accommodating high ceiling, skylights, and plenty of working space. Pipes along the ceiling are part of a fire sprinkler system.

A small garage attached to an existing home could be converted into an ideal workshop. Such a workplace offers protection from inclement weather and a means for safe and convenient tool and equipment storage. Because of a one-car garage's space limitations, workbench and cabinet/shelf storage must be designed to take advantage of all available space. This structure's attic could serve as an additional storage area for dismantled auto parts, infrequently needed accessories, and items that would otherwise clutter the work area.

This large two-stall carport could easily be converted into a garage with walls along the back and left side and a door in front. Direct access to the property's rear might be maintained by way of a third wall built on the right side about 4ft out from the house. Alternatively, a small enclosure, built where firewood is now stacked, might serve as a handy workshop/storage area in lieu of a full-blown garage remodel. For carports similar to this, take advantage of existing support posts by erecting new walls or partitions between.

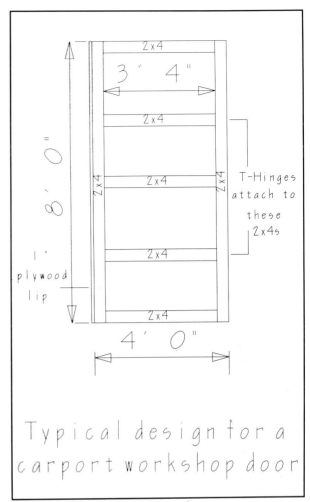

This is an easy plan for building a 4ft wide door for an enclosed carport. Vertical 2x4s are cut to whatever height your door is intended to be and the horizontal 2x4 braces are cut at 3ft, 4in; 7in will be taken up by the 3-1/2in widths of the two vertical 2x4s, and another inch is allocated for the outer plywood lip designed to strike the door stud when closed and serve as a door stop. The actual 2x4 frame width will measure 47in from outside to outside.

Work space was increased by the addition of a small carport at the front of this single-car garage. Vehicles unable to fit entirely into the garage can stick out and still be protected from rain and snow. Heavy-duty plastic secured to the carport's posts could keep blowing rain and snow from entering the outdoor work area. Note rain gutters and downspouts to channel water off the roof and keep runoff from splashing into the covered space.

Carports

A carport is simply a section of driveway that has been covered with a roof. Many homes feature them as an inexpensive means of protection against rain and snow for people moving from vehicles to their homes. Carport designs range from four-post, free-standing structures to those attached to the front or side of a house.

Basic carports can provide shade in summer and a block against rain and snow during fall and winter. Additionally, large sheets of heavy-duty plastic can be secured to open sides to prevent wind-blown rain from entering work areas. Aside from that, three important factors in converting carports into viable auto work places are: electricity and lights, solid parking surfaces, and tool storage.

Lights and Electricity

Carports without electricity can be served by way of extension cords running from household outlets to work areas. Be sure to use heavy-duty extension cords (at least 16 gauge) designed to meet the needs of power equipment like drills, grinders, and buffers. The extension cord's diameter should be at least as big as the cord attached to any electrical unit being used. Small, lightweight household extension cords designed for lamps and television sets cannot adequately carry the electrical current needed by heavier power tools. In fact, the use of light-service extension cords for large electrical appliances can cause cords to overheat to the point of shorting out and starting fires because too much current was forced through.

Extension cord length is another important consideration. In lieu of using two or three short extension cords plugged together to reach a carport work area, opt to purchase a single heavy-duty cord long enough to serve that site by itself. This helps reduce electrical resistance in the line and also decreases the likelihood of fuses blowing or circuit breakers tripping. Hardware stores and tool outlets commonly sell heavy-duty extension cords that range from 25–100ft.

Running permanent electrical service to carports should be performed by a licensed electrician. In most cases, a new circuit must be added to an existing household electrical panel in order to acquire enough power for adequate service. Only specific numbers of outlets and lights are allowed on each circuit. This ensures that excessive current is not drawn through wires when all outlets and lights on a circuit are used simultaneously. As an added safety measure, fuses or circuit breakers in electrical panels are designed to burn out or trip when excessive current is drawn. This occurs most frequently when a number of appliances and tools are used at the same time on a single circuit.

Certified electricians can determine: whether or not existing electrical panels can accommodate more circuits; which size circuits would be most appropri-

Electrical extension cords are available in a variety of styles, capacities, and lengths. The lightweight cord on the left is designed for small items like clock radios and lamps. The three-pronged, general purpose extension cord at the top is well suited for power tools like drill motors, buffers, and power washers where the distance from an outlet to the work area is 25ft or less. The 100ft, heavy-duty extension cord on the right can carry sufficient electricity over its long length without overheating or dropping current because of the wire size of which it is constructed.

Electrical wire may be purchased in bulk rolls that measure 25, 50, 100, and up to 250ft, or purchased in specific length increments from wire spools as shown here. The wire size required is determined by how far it must stretch and the amount of electrical current that will flow through it. Electric supply store employees are generally familiar with the correlation between wire size and current flow and should be able to help you choose the right wire for your custom extension cord needs. Make certain you purchase appropriately sized male and female plugs for both ends, too.

ate for specific needs; and how wires should be run to the carport—above or below ground for free-standing units, or through attics or walls for attached models. Call a few electricians to compare cost estimates, and be sure to fully explain your power needs. Will you simply want one outlet for playing a radio, or do you expect to operate heavy-use electrical tools like grinders, sanders, an air compressor, and so on?

Installing electrical outlets outdoors requires the use of special outdoor receptacles. These units are made of metal and include a cover with gasket-equipped doors for each plug. You should consider installing a number of electrical outlets around your carport area, maybe one on each support post. A box with four outlets might be handy, too. This will make it easier for you to operate more than one item without having to constantly return to an outlet to unplug one thing and plug in another.

Changing carport light fixtures from dimly lit bulbs to bright fluorescent lights is not difficult. Be certain the new lights you purchase are designed for outdoor use. Even though they may not be subject to direct rain or snowfall, moisture and cold temperatures could be fatal to some lightweight models.

When installing new lights, turn off the electricity to existing lights by way of the switch and the appropriate fuse or circuit breaker. A piece of paper at-

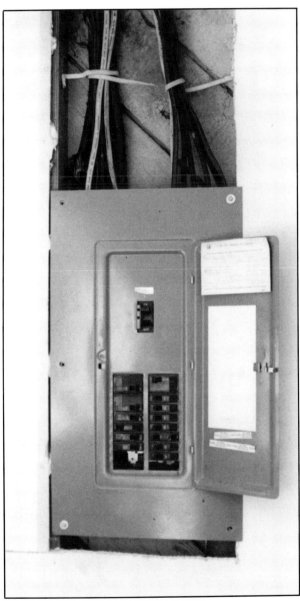

This is circuit breaker-type electric service panel. The power company's main service enters through the bottom rear of this unit to feed all of its circuit breakers. Wires going out the top of the box serve existing household outlets and light switches. Service to new outlets and light switches must come from new circuits installed in this kind of service panel box. Hire a qualified electrician to install them. Circuit breaker and wire size must be properly determined and installed to ensure safe, uninterrupted service.

Electrical outlets mounted outdoors must be protected from rain, snow, and other elements to avoid corrosion and related problems. This is accomplished by way of weatherproof outlet covers. These units are made of metal and feature spring-hinged gasket doors that keep moisture and dirt out of the receptacles. They can be purchased at electric supply stores, lumber yards, and most home improvement centers.

11

tached to the inside door of your electrical panel should describe which circuits serve which areas of your home. If not, turn on the carport lights and have someone keep an eye on them. Unscrew fuses or switch off breakers one at a time until the lights go off. The last fuse or breaker touched should be the one that serves the carport. Test this by tightening all the other fuses or switching all the other breakers to the "on" position. Then turn the actual carport light switch on and off to see if lights illuminate. If they don't, the correct fuse or breaker has been deactivated.

Slowly and carefully remove old light fixtures. Pay strict attention to how they are wired. There should be two or three electrical wires attached to them: one white; one black; and possibly one bare (ground) wire. Your new lights will have similar wires. Remember, white connects to white, black to black, and the bare ground wire to the bare ground wire. Should your carport's wiring not include a bare

third wire, read the installation instructions included with your new lights and attach ground wires to fixture-grounding screws or metal bases as indicated. Follow instructions carefully regarding light fixture mounting.

Parking Surface

A gravel carport floor is certainly solid enough to support cars and trucks, but it offers distinct disadvantages when it comes to rolling around on creepers or maneuvering floor jacks and jack stands. You can offset this by placing large sheets of heavy-duty cardboard under and around vehicles. Extra large cardboard boxes can be found at furniture and appliance stores where they are used for refrigerators, freezers, stoves, and so on. You could also place a sheet of 3/8in or thicker plywood under vehicles to offer a smooth and solid floor surface.

When using a jack and jack stands to raise and support automobiles parked on gravel surfaces, you must provide them with flat, solid bases. Blocks of wood work well. Be sure blocks are wide enough to support the entire jack or jack stand base. Provide a relatively smooth and even surface for blocks by scraping away gravel to reveal dirt.

Asphalt carport floors are much more comfortable to walk and stand on than gravel. This surface helps to keep your feet dry in rainy weather, too. Although far superior to plain dirt or gravel, asphalt has some drawbacks. Its rough texture prevents easy creeper mobility, it is susceptible to damage from spills of gasoline and other strong, petroleum-based products, and it gets very soft in hot weather—so soft that jack stands may easily penetrate asphalt to cause divots. Consequently, wood block supports should be used under jacks and jack stands operated on asphalt bases.

Asphalt is installed by contractors using special equipment and rollers. Although this material can be put down cold, most contractors prefer hot mixture applications to ensure maximum adhesion and compaction. Asphalt is generally fine for driveways and simple auto parking spaces but not a great choice for shop floors. Along with drawbacks already described, this material is difficult to keep clean. Because its surface is so rough, dirt and grit almost always remain hidden in small crevices, holes, and pockets.

Cleaning asphalt with a broom removes a great deal of debris, but a water spray is needed to thoroughly rid surfaces of most particles. This is especially important for those who plan Concours detailing, intricate machine work, or auto body and paint endeavors.

If your carport's asphalt floor is in good condition, use cardboard or plywood to accommodate creepers, jacks, and jack stands. For work requiring an environment free from dirt and grit, consider laying down a thick sheet of heavy-duty plastic over the entire floor. Park project vehicles on top of it. Secure

A new addition will extend this garage out to the footing/foundation area just in front of the square, light-colored drain under a short 2x4 board. The concrete floor will be 4in thick and reinforced with a rebar grid. The dirt base for this new floor was dug out to a depth 4in lower than the existing concrete garage floor so that the entire structure will have an identical floor-to-ceiling height. Concrete must be a minimum of 4in thick to support common passenger vehicle weights. Floors expected to support large commercial equipment or unusually heavy vehicles should be 6in thick.

the plastic sheet's edges with tape, bricks, chunks of wood, or the like. On the other hand, should existing carport asphalt suffer a multitude of large cracks, potholes, and crumbling edges, seriously consider replacing it with concrete.

Pouring a concrete carport floor does not generally cost much more than asphalt installations, and the advantages of concrete over asphalt are significant. Besides making surfaces a lot easier to maneuver on with creepers, floor jacks, and tool chests, concrete offers a very solid base for ramps, car body cradles, engine hoists and stands, transmission lifts, and almost anything else on wheels. It is easy to keep clean, too.

Concrete must be at least 4in thick to resist cracking. You may find that an existing gravel or asphalt surface will have to be dug out to a depth of 4in to accommodate a new concrete slab that will maintain the same height between floor bases and carport ceilings. This is an important consideration, especially when carport ceiling heights are limited. If possible, try to maintain at least 7ft of floor-to-ceiling opening space. Shorter working heights eliminate accessibility for many pickup trucks and other tall vehicles, as well as sufficient room for opening hoods.

Storage

Small carport workshop and storage unit combinations are fairly simple to construct. Since ceilings and floors are already in place, all one needs to do is build walls and a door. An entire unit can be made with 2x4 lumber and 1/2in or 3/4in exterior-grade plywood. Plywood ratings designate both finish smoothness and glue type—surface smoothness is indicated for each side. The letters A, B, C, and D indicate plywood surface smoothness. "A" designates very smooth plywood finishes, and "D" refers to rougher surfaces with a number of shallow knot holes and slight groove gaps. The letter "X" signals that an exterior-grade plywood glue was used to manufacture the sheet. Therefore, when purchasing plywood for an exterior building unit, make sure the letter "X" follows the finish smoothness grading letters. "CDX," for example, indicates a rather roughly finished sheet held together with exterior glue.

Plywood is also available with various grooves cut into one side to offer a more attractive siding finish. One of the most popular is "T-1-11." This style features grooves that run entire sheet lengths. They are about 1/2in wide, and spaced from 4in to 12in

The workshop on the right and the first floor section of the structure in back are each sided with "T-1-11" style, exterior grade plywood. This siding is available in a number of groove patterns, with grooves spaced from 4–12in apart.

Check lumber yards and home improvement centers to find the T-1-11 style that best matches existing home siding or offers the most appealing design.

apart. Based upon the type and style of your house's siding, T-1-11 may serve as a complimentary addition.

If you have never built a structure of any size out of 2x4s and plywood, take time to visit a construction site to see first-hand how these kinds of boards are nailed together. You may even have the opportunity to speak with carpenters who can offer handy construction tips for your project.

Basically, 2x4s are used to frame storage units, and plywood sheets are installed to enclose them. Long, pressure-treated 2x4s serve as base plates, and are bolted to the floor. Other long 2x4s are used as top plates nailed to studs and to the ceiling. Be sure you purchase enough pressure-treated 2x4s and regular 2x4s, each able to completely span the sides of your carport shop. If your unit will be 6x14ft, for example, you will need two 14ft, pressure-treated 2x4s; and two 6ft, pressure-treated 2x4s for base plates;

along with two 14ft and two 6ft regular 2x4s for top plates. Regular 8ft 2x4s will be used as *studs*, those wood frame members that run vertically between base and top plates.

Cut base and top plates to fit their intended sides. Then sandwich corresponding base and top plates together by driving nails partially into them; they will be pulled apart later. Stretch a tape measure from one end to the other and use a pencil to mark locations for studs. Studs should be placed 16in on-center from one end to the other. It is normal for the last stud to be placed closer than 16in to the end of plates when walls do not measure out in perfect, overall 16in intervals.

While making pencil marks every 16in, take time to also make pencil marks out 3/4in on both sides of 16in center lines. The distance between these two extra lines will be 1-1/2in, the exact thickness of 2x4

Building contractor Jim Yocum has already drilled holes in the bottom plate for J-bolts, marked the stud locations on both plates, and nailed together much of this wall frame using 16d sinker nails. Loose studs seen here will be nailed in and then the window header installed. It will take at least three people to tilt the wall up onto 2x4 blocks and maneuver with heavy bar levers to get it in place and over projecting J-bolts.

Note the bolt in the center of this photo secured to the middle of the bottom plate. It is attached to a J-bolt buried in the concrete floor. The wall frame was squared and covered with sheets of exterior grade plywood secured with 8d galvanized nails. This is a typical wood frame wall unit, with studs at 16in on-center. Notice the short support-stud under the edge of the window's sandwiched bottom 2x4s, right next to the regular-length stud. All headers and horizontal framing members are supported on their ends as well as their centers in this manner.

studs. This way, you will clearly recognize where each stud must be nailed to each plate.

Because each plate is 1-1/2in thick, studs will need to be 3in shorter than the opening they fit into; that 3in is filled by the plates. Now, measure the vertical opening where each wall will be placed and deduct 3in from that measurement. If the opening is 7ft 8in, for example, cut studs to 7ft 5in. Whatever the total vertical measurement, deduct 3in from it and cut each of your vertical studs to that length.

Once the 16in on-center marks have been made, separate the plates and attach studs using 16d framing nails. Put at least two nails into each stud through both the base and top plates. Start at one end of one plate and work toward the other. After the first plate has been completed, nail on the other plate. The finished wall frame should have a 2x4 stud at each end and be divided by 2x4 studs 16in on center between, except for the last stud, which very well may be closer than 16in to the final 2x4 end stud.

You can raise this framed wall into position now, or elect to nail on plywood sheathing while it is lying flat on the floor. The choice is yours, but realize that a sheathed wall will be heavier to lift and maneuver into place than one with no plywood. In either case, you must ensure that the frames are square. One way to do this is to lay a piece of plywood sheathing flat on the frame with its outside edges exactly straight and even along the outside 2x4 edges. Since plywood is milled straight and square, this method of checking squareness works quite well. Use 6d or 8d nails to secure plywood to 2x4s.

When nailing the first section of plywood in place, you will understand how important it is that studs be placed exactly 16in on-center. A plywood edge should be centered on a stud nailed at the 4ft mark along the plates. With the edge of this plywood sheet taking up only half of that 4ft-positioned stud's thickness, the next plywood edge will rest on the other half of that stud for support and nailing.

If you decided to put up frames first and then install plywood, use a 4ft carpenter's level to make sure

Yocum has already marked the J-bolt locations on this pressure-treated bottom plate. Holes will be drilled at these marks and the plate fitted over and secured to J-bolts. At this point, Yocum is measuring the distance out from the last J-bolt to determine where the plate should be cut for the new wall's length and its intersection with the front perpendicular wall.

This is a portion of an extensive home addition that incorporates a three-car-plus garage/workshop on the first floor and new living space on the second. The relatively flat roof is supported with prefabricated roof trusses, as indicated by the small metal gussets at the end of the studs. Note two top plates at the top of the wall just under the roof truss.

15

walls are positioned plumb (perfectly vertical). Secure wall ends by nailing them to carport corner posts. Check the bottom plate to see that it is level. If not, drive shims (slivers or wedges of wood) under it until it is leveled. Check the top plate as well, leveling as necessary. When level, nail walls to ceiling joists and other corner posts. Once frames are secure, measure and cut plywood to fit vertically, then nail it on.

Follow these same suggestions for all of the walls except the one which will have a door—leave it for last. With other walls nailed in place, mark a door

A new garage wall has been framed and partially sheathed with plywood. A window is framed with a 4x8 header at the top and two 2x4s doubled up at the bottom. A 2x4 brace at the front of this wall is staked to the ground and holds this wall upright until a front wall is constructed and attached. Note the black plastic pipe alongside the foundation, which will serve as a foundation and rain gutter drain line.

wall's plates as you did the others, but leave an opening for the door; no studs will fill that opening, but studs are needed on each side of it even though they may not fit within a 16in on-center rule. A good-sized door width for carport shop/storage units is about 4ft (the width of a plywood sheet).

Framing door walls is easy. In addition to studs every 16in on-center except inside door openings, you need studs on both sides of door openings for support. The stud located at the door's hinge side will be covered with plywood sheeting flush with its inside edge. The opposite stud should extend into the opening by about 1in. This will allow it to serve as a door stop. Ultimately, the horizontal opening for a full, 4ft wide door will be 3ft, 11in.

Plywood doors are framed with two long 2x4s running vertically, and four or five inserted horizontally. A door's hinge-side 2x4 should remain flush with the plywood, and the opening side should be constructed so that about 1–2in of plywood hangs over the edge of its 2x4. This lip of plywood will make contact with the wall stud that sticks out, serving as a means to stop the door in its closed position. Therefore, for a 4ft wide door, space the upright 2x4s from 3ft 10in to 3ft 11in apart from outside edge to outside edge, and allow plywood to hang over as described.

Horizontal door frame 2x4s are placed between vertical 2x4s as follows: at the top of the door; 2ft down from the top; 6ft down from the top; and at the bottom. The top and bottom 2x4s offer frame support in conjunction with the upright 2x4s, and the two 2x4s in the middle offer excellent locations for large T-hinges. These boards will have to be toe-nailed (nails driven in at an angle) together with 16d nails. Plywood is then secured with plenty of 6d nails. Just before installing the door, use a handsaw to cut off the base plate square with the studs. This allows for an unobstructed opening into the shop/storage area to accommodate rolling tool chests and other equipment.

Once your structure has been built, its interior can be outfitted with shelves, cupboards, a workbench, and so on. Consider a light over workbenches and nearby electrical outlets for power tools.

Home Garage

Many auto enthusiasts utilize their home garages as suitable auto workshops. The biggest problem, it seems, is that these spaces are also used as common storage spots by other family members. Work space is at a premium, as are locations for storing auto parts, tools, equipment, and supplies. If your garage is full of infrequently used items, you might consider moving them to a local storage facility to make more room for your automotive stuff. Or, take advantage of a warm weekend to hold a garage sale and sell unnecessary items that clutter an otherwise perfect auto work area.

Many interior walls in residential garages are not finished and expose bare stud walls. Exceptions are walls that adjoin living areas. These are covered with sheets of 5/8in thick drywall, lath, and plaster or other material as required for fire safety. Doors leading from garages to house interiors must be rated as fire doors to assist in this type of protection. Fire doors are generally solid core and equipped with self-closers.

Bare stud garage walls and ceilings should be covered with drywall or a suitable substitute. The reasons are many. Finished walls look better and will add a great deal of reflected light, especially when painted white. Insulation in walls and ceilings offers protection against cold weather and helps to reduce the amount of noise created by power tools and equipment. Workbenches and cabinets can be mounted flush to finished walls and you won't have to move them around in order to find tools and small parts accidently dropped between their rack edges and open stud spaces.

Insulation is available in 16in wide rolls perfect for insertion between studs. Backing sheets are equipped with lips that are stapled or nailed to stud faces.

Drywall sheets are 4ft wide and available in 8ft, 10ft, and 12ft lengths; they can be nailed or screwed in place. Drywall screws are easiest to insert with a variable speed drill or power driver tool. Both screws and nails must be inserted in such a way that they dimple drywall. Dimples create small pockets that hold drywall compound—a mud-like material used to cover nail or screw holes to allow for smooth, even wall surfaces. In corners and along seams, you'll need to use drywall tape along with compound. Tape and compound work together to cover gaps and seams. Exterior corners must be outfitted with metal drywall flashing to protect against bumps and keep the drywall in good condition.

Home Garage Storage

Finding places to conveniently store automotive supplies and equipment is always an important consideration. This is an area where you must be creative, especially when space is limited. Is there an attic space above your garage large enough to store boxes and other things? If your garage's attic space is open, why not consider nailing down a few sheets of 3/4in plywood to joist tops to make room for storage? In lieu of plywood, 1x4 boards may be used as reasonable attic floor material. Note, however, that lightweight, prefabricated roof trusses manufactured with

Even if your local building department does not require insulation for detached workshop structures, you should consider installing it. Insulation of varying thicknesses is available in rolls, with widths designed to fit between wall studs and ceiling joists. Small flaps on both sides of rolled insulation are easily folded out to lay on top of stud faces so they can be stapled or nailed in place. Hardware stores, lumber yards, and home improvement centers commonly stock insulation, and salespeople will help you determine appropriate "R" factors for your region and climate.

A busy, but well-organized garage space. Fluorescent lights add needed illumination, and the work space is easily capable of accommodating an automobile. Note the plain but secure 2x4 storage rack attached to the ceiling; small parts and fastener storage units on the front workbench; and equipment storage under the workbench on the right.

17

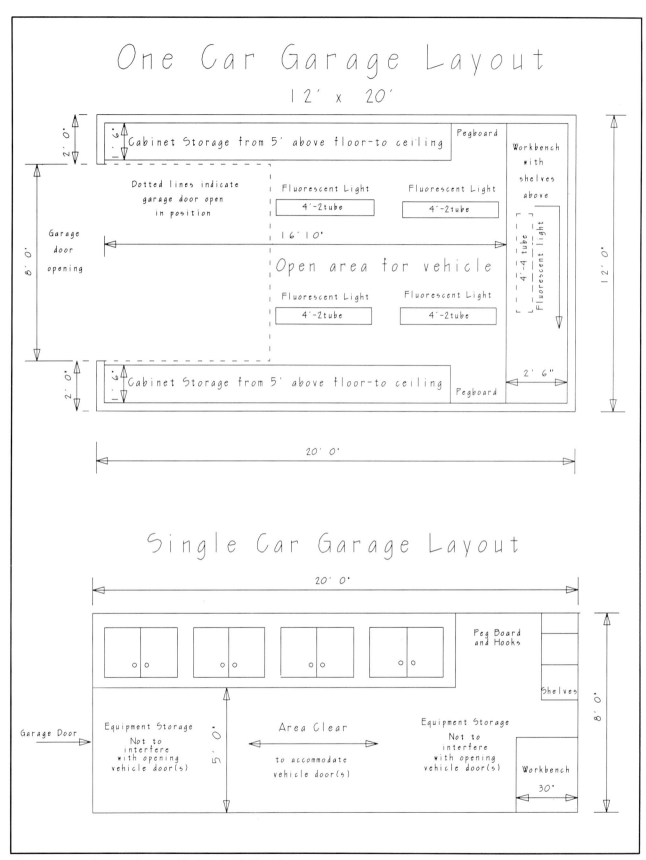

One Car Garage Layout
12' x 20'

2' 0"

9' 6"

Cabinet Storage from 5' above floor-to ceiling

Pegboard

Workbench with shelves above

Dotted lines indicate garage door open in position

Fluorescent Light
4'-2tube

Fluorescent Light
4'-2tube

4'-4 tube
Fluorescent light

8' 0"

Garage door opening

16' 10'

12' 0'

Open area for vehicle

Fluorescent Light
4'-2tube

Fluorescent Light
4'-2tube

2' 0"

9' 6"

Cabinet Storage from 5' above floor-to ceiling

Pegboard

2' 6"

20' 0'

Single Car Garage Layout

20' 0'

Peg Board and Hooks

Shelves

8' 0"

Garage Door

Equipment Storage

Not to interfere with opening vehicle door(s)

5' 0"

Area Clear

to accommodate vehicle door(s)

Equipment Storage

Not to interfere with opening vehicle door(s)

Workbench

30"

One-car garage layout, drawn with Autodesk's The Home Program.

2x4s are not designed for attic storage and may only support very light loads. Ceiling joists of 2x6 or larger lumber on 16in centers are capable of supporting much more weight.

Lumber yards and hardware stores frequently carry special attic ladder units that fold up and away into ceilings when not in use. They are spring-hinged and easily opened by pulling on a cord. Units are made in widths to accommodate spacing between ceiling joists, and you can make length openings between joists as long as desired. Along with providing an attic floor and stairway for access, be sure to drywall the entire ceiling so dust and debris will not fall from it onto active automotive projects.

Areas directly above garage doors are seldom used for anything. Consider installing a shelf or shelves along those spaces for items used seasonally, like camping gear, ski equipment, folding lawn furniture, and so on. On one side of your garage, set up a system of cupboards and cabinets for general family storage, and save the other side for automotive neces-

Sprint car mechanic Mike Holiman uses the attic above his automotive workshop for storage. Access to the space is provided by a folding attic stairway. Little effort is needed to pull down the cord and unfold this handy stairway. Spring hinges keep this unit closed, and brackets hold the staircase steady when unfolded.

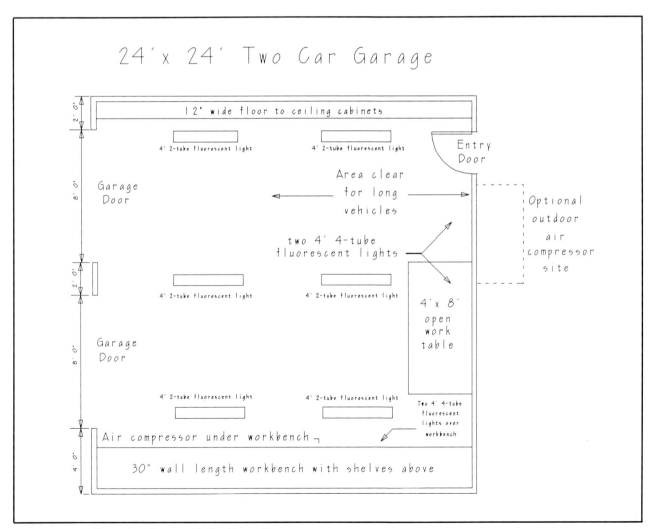

Two-car garage floor plan, drawn with The Home Program.

sities. If your garage offers more space on one side than the other, try to secure the largest side for your auto work. Vehicles are big, and the more room you have the better.

Single-car garages do not offer nearly the open space convenience of two- and three-car models. Although room on the sides is limited, small garages can be set up to facilitate a variety of auto workshop needs. Install folding workbench tables along side walls, and park vehicles only part way into garages while they are being worked on. With a standard workbench at the front, folding bench tops on side walls may offer U-shaped working spaces with lots of handy places to set tools and auto parts. A carport off the front of a garage will keep rain, snow and sunlight off of that part of your car which is exposed.

Ideally, two-car garages should measure at least 24ft by 24ft. Many times, though, standard designs are built at around 20ft by 20ft. Smaller versions do not leave much room for workbenches or storage cabinets when filled with two automobiles. This may be a problem, unless you can get by with parking only one vehicle in the garage on a regular basis. If so, use the open side as a workshop and outfit it with a workbench at the front and a system of cabinets

with working bench tops on the side. Above workbench and lower cabinets, install cupboards deep enough for hand and power tools, frequently required supplies, books and manuals, clean shop towels, and so on. Be sure to label cabinet and cupboard doors with adhesive tape strips or placards so retrieval of stored items is made quick and easy.

Auto Workshops

If you are considering the construction of a new and complete auto workshop, spend considerable time planning your overall design. Envision the types and sizes of equipment that will be included and study floor plans until you find the one that will prove the most versatile for the work you expect to undertake in the shop.

Almost every automotive professional and serious do-it-yourself enthusiast fortunate enough to work out of a bona fide auto workshop will admit that theirs just isn't quite big enough. It seems that occasions frequently crop up when another few hundred square feet would come in most handy.

Jack Holden, owner of Champion Import Service in Kirkland, Washington, says that even though his shop appears to easily accommodate three full-time

A portion of Garry Allen's 30x60ft Jags Plus auto workshop looks like this from the upstairs loft. This is one of three bays where professional Jaguar repair and maintenance is performed. Allen believes that a shop of these dimensions

should easily accommodate the needs of most serious and active auto enthusiasts. Notice how much maneuvering room is available in front of the vehicle fully parked in this 30ft deep stall.

mechanics, some extra space would be greatly appreciated once in a while. Space is especially important when large tear-down work is required for various automobiles. Where should all of the dismantled parts be stored so work operations are not obstructed or compromised?

Garry Allen, owner of Jags Plus, Inc. in Everett, Washington, has been restoring Jaguars to Concours-winning condition for many years. Business became so good that he constructed a full-scale shop in his backyard. It measures about 30ft by 60ft, and has a

loft above one end that is used as an office and parts storage facility. He says that this shop is ideal for an auto enthusiast, but he has outgrown it from a business perspective. He stresses that room for parts storage is a major concern and recommends that anyone with the opportunity to build their own auto workshop spend plenty of time analyzing and designing optimum storage spaces.

As far as Concours condition restorations are concerned, Allen knows of a number of people who have spent years researching their cars before under-

A section of Jack Holden's Champion Import Service repair garage shows a vehicle exhaust ventilation system, a large bay door and simple entry door, a two-post lift, work counter with stools, and a special ceiling insulation material that reflects heat and light back toward the floor. Although Holden acknowledges that a little extra shop space would come in handy now and again, about the only addition he wishes could be made is a floor drain system.

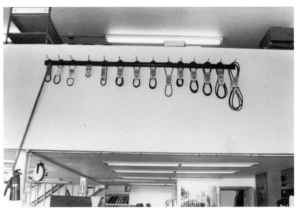

From the floor of Allen's shop, small portions of second level parts racks are visible, along with an out-of-the-way storage spot for belts. Below the loft you'll see a series of four 8ft, double-tube fluorescent lights, which offer excellent illumination.

Access to Garry Allen's automotive workshop is made along the side of his house. Fortunately, the backyard was big enough to accommodate a full 30x60ft shop and a large driveway/apron. Different-sized bay doors accommodate various vehicles, with the smallest positioned under a second story loft that serves as both an office and parts storage facility. Notice that drains are provided in front of the shop doors to prevent water runoff from entering the work space.

This area directly beneath a second floor loft is Allen's Concours preparation area. In fact, the Jaguar shown was being prepared for a Concours d'Elegance event. Along with a tremendous amount of cleaning, Concours competitors must be restored and maintained in factory-perfect condition. In order to stay abreast of all factory specifications, Allen keeps a well-stocked library filled with Jaguar manuals, bulletins, and other materials used to verify particular restoration techniques and finish standards. The library can be seen behind the vehicle's open door.

taking serious restoration projects. For that reason, he also suggests that workshops include an office area. "It doesn't have to be big, but should accommodate a desk and chair, good reading light and plenty of shelves for books, manuals, and other reference material," he says.

Mike Putnam is the manager of Mathewson's Automotive & Tire in Renton, Washington. This facility does a lot of work on high-performance, classic, and special automobiles. For his own home auto workshop, Putnam would insist upon a restroom, floor drains, and a post-type lift. He raises concerns over the practicality of center post hydraulic lifts like those

frequently seen in gas station repair bays. Their center column design obstructs many transmission removal procedures and work on center areas of most vehicles. In addition, since environmental restrictions are becoming so critically specialized, there could be a great deal of local building department concern over an underground installation of a device that contains hydraulic fluid which could possibly leak into surrounding soil.

Two- and four-post automobile lifts are constructed entirely above ground. They have safety locks which prevent vehicles from coming down unexpectedly, and include lifting arms that are out of the way

A designated office area, like Allen's, is certainly not a necessity. However, it could serve as a useful space for working up fabrication plans, developing an overall restoration schedule, conducting Concours research, and so on. A small room with good light, a book shelf, table and chair, and a door to keep dust out is worth considering, especially for those who frequently find themselves looking for a clean and quiet workshop space to read or study repair manuals or related literature.

The floor of one stall in your workshop should be perfectly flat to ensure accurate measurements while setting up chassis adjustments and major autobody rebuilding. Excepting that one flat spot, though, you should consider a slight slope toward a floor drain for freshly washed vehicles and those which just came in from the rain. A drain grate system like this is an excellent feature that allows mechanics to periodically wash their work areas with soap and water.

of most undercarriage assemblies. Four-post models allow for car doors to be opened, while some two-post models are built in such a way that opening doors is also accommodated. Post lifts can also provide temporary in-the-air parking spaces for automobiles while others are worked on beneath.

Along with contemplating shop bathrooms, drains, lifts, and office space, also consider actual working floor areas with regard to the auto work planned for your facility. Bill Snyder is a professional auto body technician for Newlook Autobody in Kirkland, Washington. His passion is building hot rods. To him, a perfectly flat floor is imperative for any auto workshop. This is needed to accommodate setting up body panels and auto chassis assemblies.

This two-post lift was installed outdoors, adjacent to a back entry door at Mathewson's Automotive and Tire, to serve as an engine and undercarriage wash rack. Thorough underbody steam cleaning is possible because the lift's arms only block meager portions of vehicle undercarriage components.

This type of center-column lift may prove useful for oil changes, chassis lubrications, wheel removals, differential repairs, and some other tasks, but limits work on all major drive train components because they are covered by the lift's support structures. Seriously envision all the tasks you plan to undertake with such a lift before purchasing and installing one in your shop. If you anticipate needs that revolve around removing transmissions and replacing clutches, you may receive better overall service from a post lift.

A short section of garden hose attached to the faucet of this old cast-iron slop sink is used to fill mop buckets and pails. Its size is generous enough to handle many parts-cleaning chores. In lieu of a new sink, you may be able to find a used one in excellent condition at surplus stores, swap meets, or sites where old buildings are scheduled for major remodeling or demolition.

Mike Holiman agrees. He has been involved with sprint cars for as long as he can remember. As the senior and chief mechanic for a sprint car crew, Holiman must have a flat and even workshop floor section. Just the slightest slope could cause him to misalign a chassis adjustment which could eventually lead to a second-place finish instead of a first. If your shop area is big enough, maybe you could accommodate a sloping floor and drain system in one area for washing and detailing, and another perfectly flat area for chassis and suspension work. The bottom line is you must determine what automotive activities will be pursued in your auto workshop and then design it to fit those needs.

Size Requirements

NO SHOP IS EVER BIG ENOUGH! Over and over again, those with an interest in restoring or repairing automobiles complain that there seldom seems to be enough room to accommodate everything that has to be accomplished in their auto workshops. Unfortunately, most auto enthusiasts are not blessed with unlimited expense accounts or lottery jackpots, nor the acreage required for the easy construction of dream facilities. However, those with the means to build auto workshops must take into account that their needs and desires may grow with time and future income.

If at all possible, build shops in such a way that additions can be easily and attractively constructed later. Along with realistic land use, be aware of footing requirements, bearing (supporting) wall construc-

tion, and roof lines. Nothing seems to make a building addition look more awkward than non-symmetrical roof lines.

Look around at houses and structures in your area. Notice how roof peaks match in one way or another. These designs are for attractiveness, of course, but serve practical purposes as well. A solid wall jutting up and over a pitched roof section will allow rain water to pool and eventually find its way under shingles to leak inside walls. Snow buildup is another concern, especially in areas where large amounts of snowfall are common. If too much snow is allowed to accumulate on roof valleys, lower snow layers might melt to surely find ways past metal flashing and down interior walls.

Roy Dunn has been professionally lettering and pinstriping all sorts of vehicles for a number of years. To better accommodate his semi-truck and trailer custom graphics trade, he had his house raised about 8ft so that an extra-tall basement workshop could be constructed. This was a major remodeling project which cost a fair sum of money. But the efforts proved most worthwhile and gave Dunn an excellent location for a variety of custom painting endeavors. For those enthusiasts with virtually unused, regular basement-sized spaces, this sort of home remodeling project may provide a viable auto workshop option.

Mike Holiman's home-based automotive workshop has been the site for a myriad of auto repairs and sprint car modifications. The concrete floor is perfectly flat so that he can accurately dial-in specific race car chassis adjustments. Although it may appear dwarfed alongside the huge fifth wheel trailer, this 24x36ft shop is easily capable of supporting almost any automotive-related task.

For engine work, one needs plenty of room at the front of shops for testing equipment, meters, gauges, and the like. For full motor dismantling, additional room must be allotted for engine hoists and stands. Auto body repair and paint work requires lots of room all around vehicles. Ideally, one should have a 10ft open space around all sides of any vehicle parked in a shop. Since many large American cars are nearly 20ft long and close to 8ft wide, this theory would call for a shop being 40ft long and almost 30ft wide—and this just for working space. What about storage?

Here again, Garry Allen's suggestion of a 30ft by 60ft shop sounds quite versatile. A shop 30ft deep should be able to easily accommodate an automobile and a 2–3ft wide workbench, and still allow plenty of working room at the front of vehicles. A 20ft depth is too shallow for most full-sized cars and a workbench, although mid- and compact-sized autos could fit and still allow a couple of feet for working room. Make it 24ft and you should have enough room to support a nominal-sized auto and a workbench with adequate working space. Remember, tool chests and rolling work carts can be moved to areas where repair or

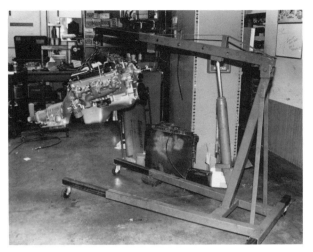

Engine hoists require lots of maneuvering room if engines are to be removed from vehicles in a controlled fashion, rather than through forceful manipulation. Therefore, try to plan an overall workshop floor area which offers lots of working space at the front of parking stalls. Likewise, determine specific storage areas where large hoists and lifts can be stored safely and out of the way of other vehicle repair spaces.

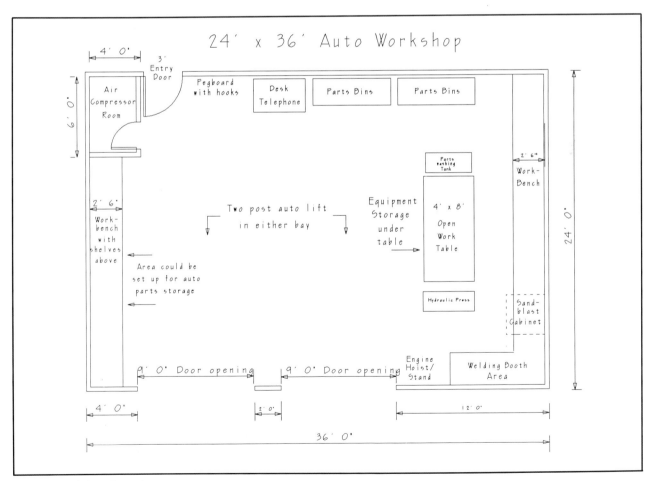

24x36ft workshop floor plan.

Every automotive workshop that stands as a separate structure (as opposed to garages attached to a home) should be outfitted with its own 200amp (minimum) electrical service panel. This supply should guarantee plenty of power to operate an air compressor, welder, and lots of other power tools and equipment. Holiman outfitted his shop with a 400amp service panel and has never experienced any electrical problems. A qualified electrician should be hired to install such devices, and your local power company will hook up actual power to the unit.

restoration work is conducted. So, if your budget or land availability cannot provide for an optimum shop width, make plans to create a versatile shop with accommodations for bringing tools and equipment to work areas in lieu of parking project vehicles amidst a plethora of stationary automotive tools and equipment.

All in all, have a master plan in mind when calculating the dimensions and designing a floor plan for auto workshops. If available land will support future service bays, be certain that walls and roof lines can be added onto later with no problems. Plan ahead for interior wall plumbing, both for water and compressed air. Instead of settling for a minimum-sized electrical service, opt for a higher 200amp or 400amp service so that additional electrical outlets can be quickly installed in the future. In other words, design your perfect auto workshop first and then build what you can at this time with the future clearly in mind. By all means, draw and write these ideas on paper. Keep working with them until you develop a plausible set of plans. Then, build your automotive workshop to include all of the amenities you can afford now, and once your overall needs and income meet at a happy medium, you'll have designs ready for the complete construction of an ultimate auto workshop.

Cost Factors

Costs for the construction of automotive workshops vary from region to region. Areas experiencing high growth and excellent economies command much higher prices than those with lower economic bases. Lumber prices have risen in recent times, as have almost all other construction materials. Building contractors, carpenters, electricians, and plumbers charge rates that are generally commensurate with their regions' economy. Regardless of locale, the least expensive way to build workshops in almost every case is to construct them yourself.

With help from a number of friends, Holiman constructed his basic 24x36ft shop in one weekend. This included walls, roof, shingles, and siding. The interior electrical and drywall work was accomplished afterward. If you know carpenters, electricians, plumbers, drywall installers, and others in building trades, attempt to trade them labor for labor. Maybe you can trade tune-ups, oil changes, and repair work on friends' vehicles for their construction expertise and labor on your shop. Or offer to help your construction friends erect buildings on their property in trade for labor on yours.

Most contractors charge by the square foot. For example, if construction costs are generally rated at $50 per square foot in your area, expect to pay about $20,000 for a 20ft by 20ft garage constructed from beginning to end without any of your personal assistance. On the other hand, you may be able to cut that cost in half by providing a major portion of the work yourself. Square foot cost estimates are almost entirely determined by geographic areas. In Taylor, Nebraska, for example, a 24ft by 30ft shop may only cost $10,000 to have built, whereas in Los Angeles it may run $40,000 and higher. Shop around and talk to a number of contractors before selecting one. Ask for references and request addresses of work already completed so you'll have opportunities to actually inspect the quality of their work.

A worthwhile alternative to a standard, wood-framed workshop is a metal building kit. A number of metal building kits are advertised at economical prices. You have to erect these structures yourself, but most kits come with thorough plans and directions. Once a concrete pad is poured, buildings are put together with screws, nuts, and bolts. After walls, roof, and doors are installed, you can outfit and use buildings as needed. When your budget allows, plan for insulation and other shop amenities.

A lot of companies advertise their metal building kits in do-it-yourself periodicals like *Popular Mechanics* and *Hemmings Motor News*. In addition, local and regional newspapers and weekly shoppers frequently carry ads from area franchise operators and independent contractors. Call a number of them for quotes on prices, structural dimensions, and available options. During off-season periods, you may be able to find dealers with fantastic price reductions. Some kits sell for as little as $2,500 for a 24ft by 24ft structure—you have to obtain appropriate permits, provide concrete slabs, and furnish all labor.

Locating Sources for Additional Ideas

Nobody is more qualified to talk about home auto workshops than avid do-it-yourself automobile

Major home and garage/workshop additions like this one can be expected to cost tens of thousands of dollars. Cost per square foot varies widely around the country. Large metropolitan contractors may charge as much as $75–$100 per square foot, while rural builders may be able to construct similar structures for $40–$50 per square foot. You may be able to offset some of these costs by doing a portion of the manual labor yourself. Better yet, try to swap your automotive labor for the construction labor of friends in the building trades.

If the high cost of typical wood frame construction taxes your automotive workshop budget to the melting point, consider alternative buildings. Cover-It Instant Garages offers a wide selection of weatherproof structures in an assortment of sizes that are easily outfitted and set up as viable

and efficient auto work and storage places. They can even be used as portable paint booths. For those auto enthusiasts on limited budgets, these structures are definitely worth investigating.

restorers and Concours winners. These folks may commonly be located through car clubs or Concours d'Elegance competitions. Serious auto restorers who win at Concours know a great deal about their specific automobile makes and models. Likewise, they know all too well how much time and effort must go into each project. To say they spend a great deal of time in their workshops is an understatement.

When people dedicate a great deal of their lives to tasks accomplished in automotive workshops, you can bet that they have invested considerable energy into making their shops viable and convenient work spaces. In addition, they most assuredly will have new ideas that could easily turn shops into dream facilities.

Very few people are able to arrive at innovative shop designs without spending lots of time working in such facilities. Those who spend lots of time in auto workshops should know how much room is required for various projects; which creature comforts would be appreciated; and what floor plans are most efficient for projects that lay ahead. Certainly, the bigger shops are the better they will serve, but if laid out awkwardly, they could turn out to be more of a hassle than they are worth.

Besides brainstorming with experienced auto restorers, professional auto technicians, and serious do-it-yourself auto aficionados, look through automotive and related periodicals. *Skinned Knuckles* is a maga-zine aimed specifically toward old car restorations. Articles in this monthly are exceptionally informative. To better assist its readership of serious restorers, *Skinned Knuckles* frequently publishes issues featuring shop ideas submitted by readers. These tips range from utilizing worn-out extension cords as holders for screwdrivers on workbench panels to making shops as functional as hospital operating arenas.

Display and classified advertisements in most auto magazines commonly feature companies that sell metal buildings, prefabricated structures, shop storage systems, tool and equipment accessories, ventilation equipment, lifts, stands, and a lot more. Call or write these companies for more information. Whether their products fit your needs or not, their informative brochures and literature could help you to determine just what designs will work best for your needs.

By all means, take plenty of time to plan your structure before digging dirt, pouring concrete, and pounding nails. Think about next year and the years ahead. What are your automotive ambitions? Do you expect to restore Concours winners, or simply maintain personal automobiles? Will your needs require a substantial auto parts storage facility? Paint booth? Suspension alignment system? State-of-the-art engine diagnostic machine? Build your automotive workshop with the future in mind. Make it work for today, but don't overlook tomorrow.

CHAPTER 2

STRUCTURAL CONCERNS

Structurally sound foundations, floors, walls, and roofs are paramount to protect and support any accessories inside buildings, especially inside automotive workshops. After all, what good is a shop building if it leaks during rain storms and cannot withstand a few gusts of wind without falling over?

To a great degree, national building codes were developed to help ensure that building designs and their structural integrities meet specific standards of strength and general safety. These building codes and guidelines were implemented to help people learn how to construct strong buildings, not only for their own protection, but also for the protection of others, such as neighbors, visitors, and passersby.

To further guarantee that buildings are constructed according to approved standards, most city and

The ceiling and roof covering Holden's Champion Import Service was constructed with glue laminated beams, commonly referred to as glue-lams. Two of them can be seen at the ceiling in this photo, next to the fluorescent lights. Glue-lams consist of a series of 2x4 or 2x6 lumber milled perfectly and then glued together. They can support great weight without the need for post supports, making them perfect for wide spans. Guides at lumber yard service centers explain which glue-lam sizes are designed for specific spans.

county governments maintain active building department divisions. These building departments are responsible for the approval of construction plans. They note initial design problems so that builders can make early adjustments in order to finalize their plans' approval and begin building projects. Once plans are approved, building inspectors must be called out to inspect various construction activities to ensure they are accomplished according to code.

Although some do-it-yourselfers may regard any type of governmental restriction as an infringement upon their freedom, a more realistic attitude acknowledges that building departments simply want to ensure that structures are built soundly for the protec-

tion of owners and everyone else.

To that end, check with your local building department before starting any construction project. Many offer handouts which clearly show recommended dimensions for footings, foundations, and wall sizes, joist and rafter dimensions for specific spans, and so on. Additional information should help guide you through the permit and inspection process

1x4 boards are nailed on top of 2x8 lumber to make footing forms. The 1x4s were cut 19in long to offer a 16in inside width between 2x8 forms; the additional 3in is found in the width of the two 2x8 boards, which are each 1-1/2in thick. Finished forms offer a footing area 16in wide and 8in deep,

following the building department code for the garage/workshop addition. A long level is used to ensure that footing forms are placed flat, and a string is used as a guide to set forms in line with the existing structure. Foundation wall forms will be attached to this footing form base.

so that actual construction progresses without interruption.

Footings and Foundations

Although the terminology for footings and foundations may differ in various regions, the structural significance of these units is the same. For all intents and purposes, *footings* are generally regarded as troughs filled with concrete and designed to support walls. Footings almost always start at ground level and extend below grade to specified depths based on the types of structures intended to be built on top of them, the region's climate, and the likelihood of such occurrences as earthquakes. For example, footings for two-story and taller structures will be wider and deeper than those for single-story buildings.

Foundations are basically concrete or cement block footing extensions. They rise from ground level to the point where walls begin. Foundations ensure that walls are not built at ground level, in order to help eliminate problems associated with moisture accumulation and dry rot in wood walls. You may notice that common household garages incorporate short, concrete *stub* walls which extend from a floor

Many home garages feature short stub walls around their perimeters. These foundation walls keep dirt and water out of garages that would normally have floors placed at ground level—a step or two down from a home's first floor. Contractors generally pour footings and foundations first, strip their forms, and then pour garage floors a week or two later. This short stub wall section is located next to a roll-up garage door, and evidence that the floor was poured after the wall was in place is seen as a dark concrete splatter on the face of the wall.

A three-car-plus garage/workshop with new living space on top is a major construction project. Designs must follow building code specifications in order to ensure structural stability. Since a stairway is planned for this area, a glue-lam could not run to the wall on the right. Therefore, its end must be supported by a post. Note the concrete foundation walls, which also serve as the footings/foundation for the existing house, as well as retaining walls to hold back dirt.

The existing footing and foundation for this old garage is unusually thick and deep, poured that way years ago to compensate for a sloping drop-off. Notice that the new footing form extends past the old one so that a foundation wall can be formed in the center of the footing and in line with the structure's existing wall. A newer concrete slab was poured around the existing walls a number of years ago, and will require new concrete to fill the gap once the wall section is removed to accommodate the new addition. The thin concrete lip by Yocum's left hand is only 1-1/2in thick, part of a slab that was poured over the original floor years ago. It will be cut out along with the bottom plate next to Yocum's right hand so that new concrete will join the existing concrete floor in a straight and level fashion.

With a footing form positioned flat and perpendicular to the existing structure, foundation wall forms are now being installed. For the exterior foundation wall form, sheets of 3/4in plywood were cut at specific widths that will span the distance from the top of footing form 1x4s to the level of a new garage/workshop concrete floor. The interior foundation wall forms will be 4in shorter, as the footing, foundation, and slab will all be poured at the same time. No stub walls will be featured on this new addition so its floor and walls can match the existing garage. The footing and interior foundation forms will be buried in concrete; only exterior foundation forms will be stripped a few days after the pour.

to the *sole* (bottom) plate—the 2x4 or 2x6 board, laid flat at the bottom of wood frame walls, to which upright studs are attached.

Some concrete floor designs incorporate both footings and foundations in one unit. This is accomplished by forming floors so that a concrete surface will rest at least 6in above existing grade. Although a solid concrete footing/floor design may be suitable for many construction sites, sloping grades and the need for lower floor heights may require stub walls so that an actual floor level can be more in line with an existing structure or better accommodate driveway grades and the need for maximum shop ceiling height.

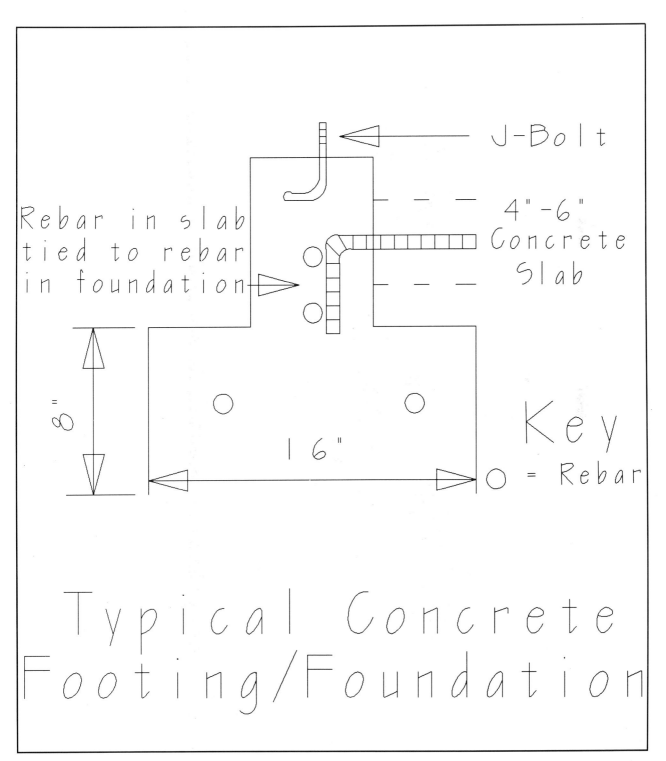

J-Bolt

Rebar in slab tied to rebar in foundation

4"-6" Concrete Slab

8"

16"

Key

O = Rebar

Typical Concrete Footing/Foundation

Floors

Concrete is the most common material used for auto workshop floors. Poured correctly, concrete is strong, stable, and very long-lasting. Liquid concrete sealers, applied to surfaces after concrete has set up, will help resist stains from oil leaks and other spills.

Concrete garage and workshop floors are generally poured after footings and foundations are in place. Although slabs must be at least 4in thick to offer any real stability, many shop owners prefer 6in thick slabs to better support heavier vehicles.

To help concrete slabs maintain a high degree of strength and resist cracking, many building departments require the installation of reinforcing rebar (steel rod) into footings, foundations, and slab areas. Rebar is placed in grid patterns, with each rebar intersection held together by tie wire or a tack weld. In lieu of rebar for slabs, you could use 6x6in number 10 wire mesh. Also referred to as *hog wire*, it comes in rolls 7ft wide and up to 100ft long. Both rebar and hog wire may be cut to length at lumber yards, some home centers, or the concrete batch plant where it is purchased.

A strip of the original concrete poured for this old garage has been exposed after the 1-1/2in lip of newer concrete was chipped out. Original J-bolts were bent over with a sledge hammer, and rebar has been inserted into holes drilled into the original foundation in preparation for a new concrete slab for a new garage/workshop addition. Notice that the old bottom plate has been removed and that the exterior foundation form for the new slab rises about 4in above the slab area to be level with the existing garage floor.

Rebar is typically sold at lumber yards; specific diameters are required for various structural footings and foundations. Rebar is suspended in the middle of footings by tie-wire wrapped around 1x4s or other pieces of rebar that run across the tops of forms. A grid system of rebar in the middle of concrete slabs offers a great deal of stability and helps to prevent cracking. Notice that all rebar sections and ends that intersect with others are secured tightly together with tie-wire. The drain (under a short 2x4) has been placed at an angle to accommodate water runoff. The new garage structure will end at the footing/foundation. Concrete poured past that point will slope toward the drain.

Moisture infiltration is a major shop concern. If moisture wicks its way up through floors from the ground beneath, it will attack auto undercarriages and begin the rusting process. To help eliminate this problem, pour concrete slab floors directly on top of thick sheets of heavy-duty plastic. You might also check around with various lumber yards to see if they carry any other type of *vapor barrier* that will surpass the abilities of plastic to hold back moisture and cold temperatures. Vapor barriers are exceptionally important in areas subject to long wet winters, and in those lowland areas with frequently damp ground soils.

Auto workshop floors do not always have to be constructed with concrete. For shops that must be built over the side of small slopes, you can use *car decking*. Essentially, car decking consists of thick, 2x6in tongue and groove lumber nailed to a supporting framework of heavy post and beam timbers. Since this type of floor must be designed and constructed to support a great deal of weight, you must follow specific building code post- and beam-spacing and span-dimensions closely. In an extreme case where a shop is planned to cantilever over open areas, hire a certified building engineer or architect to design and develop building plans.

The concrete footing, foundation, and slab for a new garage/workshop addition has been poured and finished. Note the J-bolts sticking up along the sides, and an exterior drain flush with the concrete surface. The swath of lighter-colored concrete running from left to right (just inside the end form and over the drain) indicates a broom finish. A soft push broom was swept over this outdoor area while the concrete was wet to give that part of the concrete finish a rougher texture which will improve traction. With the old 1-1/2in concrete lip cut out, the new concrete slab blends well with the existing garage floor.

Concrete footing, foundation, and slab forms are generally held together or secured to stakes with double-headed (duplex) nails. The nail's first head makes contact with wood and the second sticks up so nails can be pulled out to facilitate the removal of forms a few days after concrete has been poured. Duplex nails are available in different sizes. The 16d size is good for heavy form lumber, as shown here, while an 8d size is most suitable for regular wood stake and form work.

Car decking is basically 2x6 or larger lumber milled with tongue and groove edges. Boards fit tightly together to offer extra strength for wooden floors that are destined to support heavy loads. Although a majority of auto workshop/garage floors are poured in concrete at ground level, some structures must be built to cantilever above ground to compensate for sloping grades. Car decking must be supported by heavy timber posts and beams placed according to architectural plans.

Walls

Common workshop walls are generally constructed with 2x4 boards placed on 16in centers. Since the advent of environmental concern over heat loss and the waste of energy, many regions now require exterior walls for new construction to be built with 2x6 studs on 16in centers, to allow more room for insulation. Again, you must check with your local building department for current details. Mike Holiman installed 2x6 exterior wall studs in his shop, and noted that the extra insulation placed in them helps to keep his shop warmer in winter and cooler in summer.

Wood frame walls are attached to foundations by way of J-bolts. These anchors are set into wet concrete poured for foundations. They are inserted at intervals previously determined, and marked by nails partially pounded into forms. Generally, J-bolt anchors are placed about 1ft inside every corner and then about every 3ft or so along wall lengths. You must determine where studs and doors will be placed along exterior walls first, and then decide where J-bolts can go so they do not end up in the middle of studs or doorways.

J-bolts are mandatory for the construction of any wood frame wall on top of a concrete or block foundation. They are used to secure walls to floors, and their locations must be well planned. Before concrete is poured, determine J-bolt locations and clearly designate those sites with nails partially driven into outside form faces. J-bolts should be lo- cated between studs and not in the middle of doorway openings. To determine exactly where holes need to be drilled in bottom plates, lay pressure-treated boards in position next to J-bolts and use a square to make straight pencil marks even with each bolt's edge. Drill holes in the middle of the boards between the two pencil lines.

Some contractors prefer to nail studs to a pressure-treated bottom plate directly, nail on a top plate, and then raise framed walls into place up and over J-bolts. Others prefer to secure bottom pressure-treated plates to J-bolts first, frame walls with regular (not pressure-treated) bottom plates, and then nail walls to pressure-treated bottom plates already secured in place with J-bolts.

Tops of studs are held together with *top plates*, regular 2x4 or 2x6 lumber laid flat on top of studs. Most wood-framed structures utilize two top plates. The first one is nailed directly onto studs, and then

On occasion, J-bolt installation may be overlooked or simply impossible to accommodate at the time concrete is poured. In those situations, anchor bolts are used in lieu of J-bolts. Holes in concrete are made with a rotary hammer power tool and special concrete bit. A few different types of anchors are available at hardware stores and lumber yards. Next to the rotary hammer is a lag bolt and shield combination. Specific-sized holes are drilled in concrete to accommodate the particular shield size; shields are tapped into holes; and then their matching lag bolts are screwed into them. As bolts are tightened, the lower portions of the shields are forced outward to secure them in the hole. Other types of anchoring bolts are one-piece units that are simply tapped into holes without shields. A wedge-shaped ring at the base is forced out as the unit's nut is tightened against a board.

The single top plate on this wall will be joined by a second top plate once all walls are constructed and raised into position. In this case, a second top plate will run along the top of the wall on the left to cover and better secure the right wall to it. In other words, all seams where first top plates butt adjoining walls will be covered with a second top plate to tie the walls together.

A short 2x4 brace is temporarily secured to studs in preparation for the installation of a glue-lam. Once the beam is in its approximate position on the brace, as indicated by a string level, a long 4ft level will be used to ensure it is perfectly level before nailing. Short studs placed inside the taller ones support the glue-lam, while short studs on the outside support garage door opening headers. To ensure plenty of structural strength before ceiling joists and rafters are installed, gaps between large door headers and the top plate are filled with 2x4 lumber, and walls are sheathed with plywood. Because attic storage space was desired, this roof will be stick framed with 2x6s on top of a glue-lam instead of being outfitted with prefabricated 2x4 roof trusses. Notice that ceiling joists overlap each other on top of the glue-lam and are braced with 2x6 blocks between them.

walls are raised into position. Once all the walls are raised and secured plumb by way of support boards and stakes, second top plates are nailed on top of the original ones to tie all of the walls together. This is especially important for long walls where single top plates are not long enough to extend full wall lengths. A second top plate is centered over breaks in the first plate to add support and strength.

Fire stops are short 2x4 or 2x6 boards (depending upon which size lumber is used for walls) nailed horizontally between studs, about midway between bottom and top plates. They add some stability to walls and also help to prevent fire from extending from a lower part of a wall to the top. They may be required by your building department, so be sure to carefully read all instructions given to you by building department personnel.

Door and Window Framing

Because doors and windows are wider than 16in, a brace must be installed above their openings to support the weight of roof structures. These braces are called *headers*. Header sizes are determined by window/door widths, wall heights, roof designs, and bearing weights put on those sections of wall. Some headers can be as small as 4x6, while others must be at least 6x12. Wider spans require heavier timbers. A 4ft wide window opening, for example, may only require a 4x6 header, whereas a 10ft door opening might call for a heavy-duty 6x12 beam.

Headers are framed into walls at the same time as, and along with, studs. The easiest way to accomplish this task is to nail both the top and bottom plates together. Stand them on their sides and use a pencil to mark the location of studs (16in on center), as well as the openings for doors and windows. Note what is supposed to go where on the plates.

Shorter studs must be nailed under each end of the headers for support. This means that the true opening for a door or window will be measured between those shorter studs that hold up the header. Do not cut headers to actual door or window lengths—make sure headers are at least 3in longer than actual openings. This extra 3in is made up by the width of both the shorter studs; 2x4 and 2x6 lumber actually measure only 1-1/2in thick. Keep in mind that even though smaller headers may only require one short stud on each end, larger headers, like 6x12s, may require two or three studs on each end.

Doors and windows are available in a variety of sizes and styles. It is best to decide which sizes and brands you plan to install before framing openings for them. Most door and window manufacturers specify exactly what size to make rough frame openings so they will accommodate their products. The rough opening sizes commonly specified for doors and windows generally allow some extra room for final adjustments. These finish carpentry tasks are accomplished with small shims made out of scrap wood.

Rough framed window and door openings should be made slightly larger than actual window or door sizes. The extra room allows windows and doors to be maneuvered into perfectly level and upright positions by use of shims. Instructions that accompany window and door units will normally indicate specific rough framing dimensions. Gaps between inside window and door edges and rough framing studs are covered with wood trim and moulding.

39

A typical window installation starts with a rough framed opening lined with heavy-duty house wrap material secured with staples. Jim Woodcock and Matt Jacobs maneuver a window in its opening as shims are placed under the window frame inside the shop to help keep the unit level. Shims are simply small pieces of scrap wood used to hold window frames level until they are nailed in place. Some window frames feature pre-drilled holes for nails, while others are simply nailed through. Wood trim and moulding will fill interior gaps between windows and studs, and regular siding will cover exterior window frame flanges.

Roofs

Wood roof structures can be built in two basic ways: *stick framed;* or *trussed.* Stick framing requires the individual placing and nailing of 2x6 boards in place as *ceiling joists* and *rafters.* Roof truss designs are much easier and quicker to install because the joists and rafters are engineered and built together as

Stick framed *roof structures are built utilizing separate boards nailed together systematically. Truss roofs are quickly installed by nailing and securing prefabricated trusses that incorporate both ceiling joists and rafters in units secured together with gusset plates. Stick framing requires specific angle end cuts on rafters to ensure proper slope from a ridge pole down to walls. Trusses are manufactured*

according to the roof height and span dimensions provided on building plans. Where 2x4 trusses are quick and easy to install and usually do not require post supports, stick framed 2x6 and larger ceiling joists and rafters supported by glue-lams or posts and beams normally offer more weight-bearing capacity to accommodate greater attic storage volume and weight.

units by manufacturers. Because of the engineering and the amount of bracing built in, most common roof trusses are made out of 2x4 lumber. Each roof truss is stood up and then nailed in place, generally on 2ft centers. Plywood sheathing is then nailed to them and covered with roofing paper and shingles.

Many lumber yards are equipped to construct roof trusses. Others generally know where such components can be ordered and purchased locally. A special truck is used to haul trusses to work sites, as they are much too big to be carried conventionally on flatbed trucks or pickup lumber racks. In special cases, small cranes are employed to raise and place roof trusses on top of secured walls.

It is imperative that truss makers are given exact dimensions and appropriate delivery information at the time orders are placed. Builders must know what distance trusses must span, how far their tails are expected to stick out past exterior walls to make eaves, and what kind of pitch is desired.

Roof pitches are expressed in inches of vertical drop per foot of horizontal run. A four-in-twelve, for example, means the roof pitch falls 4in for every 12in of horizontal run. Steep pitches are difficult to walk and work on, especially while shingling. On the other hand, steep roof pitches make for generous attic storage spaces. In most cases, auto workshop roofs are made to look just like the roofs of surrounding houses.

Roof pitch is designated by how many inches a roof slopes per foot of its horizontal run. Typical pitches are generally about a 4in or 5in drop per foot of run. This roof construction feature is predetermined for add-on structures, as the addition's roof should match the one on an existing structure. However, the pitch on a new, detached building can be as great as desired, according to preference and the amount of attic storage space needed; highly pitched roofs offer the greatest amount of attic space. This roof will be skip-sheathed with 1x4 boards and then covered with cedar shake shingles. Plywood is used over the eaves. It extends inward about 2ft to ensure adequate structural strength.

If your workshop roof's design does not have to match the roof on your house, you may consider stick framing it at a steep pitch with 2x6 or larger lumber. Do this to accommodate extra attic storage. Joist and rafter sizes are determined by the distances they must span. The bigger the lumber, the farther it can span. In addition, if you plan to store a lot of heavy automotive parts in an attic, the roof will need heavy lumber to support the added weight.

Second story floor joists are usually constructed with 2x10 lumber, assuming the spans will not exceed 12ft. Specific codes spell out which size lumber is required for specific applications, and you must determine this before submitting plans. A building department official should be able to guide you to books offering this information.

As an example, let's say a shop will measure 30ft wide by 40ft long. The peak of its roof will run parallel with the 40ft walls and, therefore, joists and rafters will have to span a distance of 30ft. Roof trusses can easily be made to span that space without need for supports in the middle. However, your storage capability will be limited to little if any weight or bulk. Stick framing such a building with 2x10s might have to include a post and beam support that runs down the middle of the shop.

A beam presents little difficulty as it will be mostly located in the attic, but you might have to install a couple of 6x6 or 8x8 posts from the floor to the beam for required support. Although you may not like the thought of having a couple of posts in the middle of your shop, you will gain almost a complete second floor for parts storage. A very solid floor can be made by covering 2x10s with 3/4in plywood. The steep pitch might give you as much as 6ft of headroom in the center of your attic.

Stick framing roofs will require rafters to be cut at various intricate angles. One end of each rafter must be cut at an angle which corresponds to a specific pitch so it will butt flush against the ridge pole high above the center of the structure. In some cases, especially with additions onto existing buildings, rafter ends that rest on top of walls must` be notched in order to blend in with the slope and level of older roofs.

Many roofs, both stick framed and trussed, are sheathed with plywood and then covered with roofing paper and shingles. However, roofs covered with cedar shake shingles are skip-sheathed with 1x4 boards instead of plywood. A slender 1x4 or other wood section is placed next to nailed boards and used as a spacing guide. At the roof top next to a ridge pole, solid rows of 1x4s are installed for added strength and support. Skip-sheathing is covered with roofing paper and then with cedar shake shingles. Shingle gaps are purposely offset to prevent solid streams of water runoff and reduce mold and mildew accumulations. Shingles for the very top parts of roofs along angled ridge pole sections are units designed especially for this application.

The configuration of workshop roofs is an important concern. Along with attractiveness, you must consider practicality and the need for additional storage space. If you are not familiar with building construction and haven't a clue as to what type of roof you want, talk to an architect or professional building contractor. This is not an area that can be changed over and over again once construction starts. Trusses cannot be altered in any way, and stick framing must be done according to code so that roofs will hold up under adverse weather conditions, especially heavy snowfalls.

Skylights

Roof openings that allow natural sunlight into shops have distinct advantages and disadvantages. Obviously, skylights help to brighten shop areas and increase visibility inside them. A few skylight models include panel opening features that allow hot, stuffy air and pollution to flow up and out. Some people like skylights for the increased light and ventilation they afford, while others frown heavily upon them.

Besides the fact that skylights create a rather easy entry for thieves, some auto enthusiasts do not like them because they allow sunlight to shine directly on specific items in their shop. Excessive exposure to ultraviolet rays can ruin auto upholstery, paint, vinyl tops, and many other things. If the locations of skylights and a number of vulnerable shop items are incompatible, then maybe skylights are not for you. Such cases might include shops where a lot of body and paint or upholstery work is conducted. Others might involve the storage of classic, restored, or special automobiles.

Although most skylights can be covered with films that are supposed to filter out ultraviolet light, one can never be sure that this protection is sufficient for a Concours quality vehicle. Conversely, should storage of an expensive restoration not be in the plans for the shop you are building, you may find skylights an excellent addition. By all means, carefully consider all of the ramifications of installing skylights in your shop. Would skylights become a point of easy entry for thieves on your particular roof? Can direct sunlight damage specific parts, tools, or equipment? Would just one skylight above a workbench serve you well by lighting only that area for optimum visibility of small assembly work?

Doors

Regular household garage doors generally measure about 8ft wide and 7ft high for single models, and 16ft wide by 7ft high for doubles. Seriously consider what types of vehicles will be going in and out of your shop before purchasing over-the-counter garage doors and before framing your shop. There are plenty of companies around supplying larger doors, which your structure must be built to accommodate.

In essence, tall doors require taller shop walls. This is because a large header has to be installed over the door opening during the wall framing phase. If you need a 10ft high door to allow entry of a motor home or large truck, then the walls and ceiling of your shop must be made taller than the normal 8ft standard household garage. This will require taller studs, too.

Along with lots of other considerations, you should spend time deciding the most beneficial dimensions for bay doors. Although your shop's ceiling height may be factored at a suitable level, you must remember that large headers will extend down from the ceiling to the tops of door openings, making actual door heights lower than the adjoining ceiling's. Most residential single-car garage doors measure about 7ft high and 8ft wide, and two-car garage doors 7ft high by 16ft wide. Standard doors are generally available in 8, 10, and 12ft heights, with widths that range from 8–20ft. Door opening widths will determine header sizes, which also factor into overall door height possibilities. Measure the tallest vehicles that will most frequently be driven into your shop to determine a desired door height, then go from there to accurately determine how to accommodate that need with regard to shop ceiling height, header dimensions, and so on.

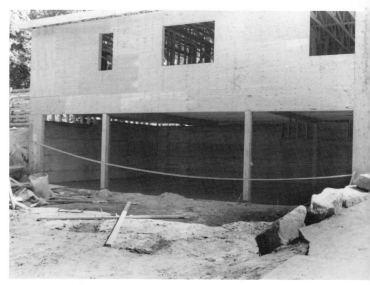

Since Garry Allen's auto workshop was built as a two-story structure with a second floor loft only covering half of the building, a tall ceiling at the far end of the shop could accommodate a tall bay door. Conversely, only a nominally sized door would fit under the loft. For garage/shops designed with living spaces above that must be built to match existing home designs, door height size may be restricted to specific dimensions, whereas width openings might be adjusted to suit specific needs. The addition in this case can be outfitted with a wide double door in the center and regular 8ft wide single doors on the sides.

If you have poured tall foundation stub walls, say 2ft, then you might be able to frame the shop with standard 8ft walls and still have an opening that can accommodate a taller door. This is because the floor-to-ceiling height will measure close to 10ft (2ft stub wall plus an 8ft framed wall), and the door header will only extend down to around 8-1/2–9ft from the floor. Before calculating the relationship between stub and framed walls to gain a larger door access, talk to a garage door company representative to see what size doors are standard. Standard doors made on a regular basis cost much less than custom doors made to fit specific openings.

Along with a large door or doors for your vehicles, plan to install a small, people-sized entry door. This is a very handy item for almost every shop. Without one, you and everybody else will have to open a big door every time someone wants in or out. In the summer this may not cause much of a problem, because the door(s) will probably be open anyway. In winter, though, you may not appreciate somebody opening up a big door and letting all of the heat out and cold in.

Rough bay/garage door openings, outlined with just studs and a header, must be built according to rough opening dimensions specified in directions accompanying the doors which will ultimately be installed. These dimensions can also be found in lumber yard manuals. Before doors are installed, their openings are trimmed with 2x6 or larger premium grade lumber to finish the appearance; this trim feature is calculated into the rough opening door dimensions. Once door trim and structure siding is installed, caulking is applied to gaps and seams to prevent water infiltration.

A three-block tall foundation wall around the base of Bill Snyder's auto workshop enabled the builder to use regular 8ft 2x4 studs to construct walls that would lead to a 10ft high ceiling. This added ceiling height also allowed for tall bay doors. The roof was constructed with trusses that span the entire shop width to alleviate any need for post supports in the middle of the shop.

Shop Height

Have you ever tried pulling an engine in a shop or garage with a ceiling so low the hoist could not be raised to its full extension? Or to conduct body and paint work on the roof of a 4x4 pickup when there was only a foot or so of clearance between it and the ceiling? Not too accommodating, was it?

As a general rule of thumb, active auto restorers and enthusiasts believe 10ft ceilings are adequate for most purposes. This height should allow plenty of room for the use of engine hoists, utility booms, and some small lifts. Once again, you have to envision what kinds of activities may occur in your shop in order to accurately design wall and ceiling heights that will best serve those needs.

Some enthusiasts, like Ron Weglin, of Harrah's Automotive in Seattle, Washington, believe that ceilings must be at least 12ft high to accommodate full-

A 10ft tall door was required for Dunn's new shop to accommodate extra large trucks and other vehicles slated for custom lettering, pinstriping, and graphics. To facilitate this extra-tall door and shop ceiling, Dunn's entire house was raised a number of feet above its original foundation and repositioned on top of a newly constructed, taller one.

After the installation of a two-post auto lift in their shop, Rick and Ron Weglin wished the ceiling was just a foot or two taller to accommodate open hoods on vehicles raised to full lift height. In lieu of a complete shop remodel, they opted to cut a chunk out of the ceiling drywall to make space for hoods. As a fire safety measure, all wood surfaces within an opening like this should be covered with a layer of 5/8in drywall.

size lifts. For example, you may plan to include a four-post lift in your shop that will double as an elevated parking space for a car while work is completed on another underneath. In that case, you will need a ceiling height that will allow the lift to raise the parked car to its maximum height. If that lift can raise cars 6ft off of the ground, and the car parked on it is 5ft tall, it stands to reason that the shop's ceiling must

Tall, wide doors provide plenty of space for large vehicles to enter Dunn's commercial graphics, pinstripe, and lettering facility. Posts in the center of the structure support a large beam which runs down the middle of the ceiling. Since Dunn has no need to raise vehicles on a lift, this ceiling height is adequate for work on semi-trucks and other large vehicles.

be at least 11ft high. In that situation, a 12ft ceiling would be more appropriate.

This goes for other lifts as well, even though they may not be used for additional parking. What if you wanted to fully raise a macho 4x4 with giant tires and a beefy suspension? Does that vehicle stand 6ft, 7ft, or taller? Will you need a 14ft ceiling for its complete clearance, or more? Maybe those shops outfitted with lifts and used for 4x4 or tall vehicle maintenance should be designed as full, two-story units, having a partial second floor for parts storage and the rest fully open, with an expansive cathedral ceiling that offers a 20ft clearance.

Naturally, the cost to construct a two-story shop building will be greater than that of a single-story design. Likewise, building department regulations may limit structures to specific heights, and your actual needs may only call for a single-story design. Therefore, for all practical purposes, plan for a ceiling height of at least 8ft. Anything shorter will most likely hinder a number of shop activities, from fully raising hoods and opening convertible tops, to working on roofs and maneuvering large body panels.

Shop Security

Mike Holiman's shop has no windows or skylights. He built it this way on purpose, and would do it again in a second. Why? Security. He figures that if nobody can peek in through windows to see what kinds of tools and equipment he has in his shop, then nobody will bother breaking in. It must be true, as he has had no problems whatsoever with theft or vandalism. He prefers to have tools and equipment displayed out in the open for easy access, and likes the option of just closing the shop doors after working on a project without having to put everything out of sight for the night.

One of the main reasons auto enthusiasts erect viable workshops is to have places where tools, equipment, auto parts, and other items can be safely and conveniently stored. It does not take long to amass a small fortune in these things, and your insurance company may not place the same dollar value on them as you do. Their loss could be devastating, especially if some items, like classic parts, are virtually irreplaceable.

Although windows and skylights might offer additional light and ventilation, you must consider their location and vulnerability to burglar access. Are windows planned close enough to ground level that someone could easily break them and climb through? Could a determined thief climb onto your shop's roof and gain access through a big skylight? Is your shop located in an area where the probability of such crimes is real? These are very valid concerns which you must consider when designing your shop building.

Should you adamantly desire windows in your shop and also want to maintain as much security as possible, plan to install wide windows with narrow openings as high up on walls as possible. Narrow windows are very difficult to climb through, much less carry items out of, and their placement at the top of walls should require a ladder for any thief who wants to look through them. Consider opaque glass like that used for bathroom windows. On sliding windows, cut sections of 3/4in dowel to fit in the rails and block the movement of sliding panels toward their opening sides. Look around at hardware stores and home improvement centers for devices designed to secure sliding windows, and install them as added security measures.

Burglar alarms, outdoor spotlights that automatically turn on when moving objects are detected, and guard dogs are some means employed by auto workshop owners to maintain security—none of which are completely foolproof. If your shop is out in the country, who will hear a burglar alarm or notice an illuminated spotlight if you are not home? How dependable are guard dogs? Are you willing to maintain vicious guard dogs that may prove more of a liability to you and your family than security against burglars? Overall, Holiman might have the best idea—*out of sight, out of mind.*

Another security point you should consider is the actual storage of tools, equipment, and parts. Should you maintain them on open shelves and hangers, or keep them stored inside cabinets and cupboards? For the most part, this depends on how you expect to utilize your shop. Do you plan on frequently selling various automobiles and parts out of your shop, or hold open car club meetings there? Do large bay doors open onto a busy street? These are situations where strangers might have ample opportunities to observe your shop's inventory. Unfortunately, there are unscrupulous people around who take advantage of such opportunities to case various locations for the sole purpose of robbing them.

Should any of the above scenarios relate to your shop, be sure to design it in such a way that the majority of tools and equipment are kept out of view of open bay doors, and stored behind locked cupboards and cabinets when not in use. To facilitate tool access and usage during work activities, employ rolling carts for their transport from the tool storage area to the actual work space.

Supplemental Design Considerations

At first, the simple idea of a large building set up for the express purpose of restoring or repairing automobiles is plenty exciting by itself. However, as you seriously ponder the overall use of this facility, you are sure to come up with more and more attributes that you will eventually want to include. Therefore, take plenty of time to design this structure and, by all means, talk to lots of other owners to learn what they would do differently if they could rebuild their shops from the ground up.

Before you go out and start digging footings, pouring concrete, and pounding nails, consider other related functions such as: electrical service, heating, compressed air needs, and general creature comforts. All must be accounted for in a set of building plans. Your plans must indicate such things as how the electrical service will be connected; what type of heating system will be installed; how water runoff will be routed away from the structure; and where the bathroom will be plumbed in.

Welders, air compressors, plasma cutters, and heavy-duty power tools require lots of electricity. Simply running a couple of small electrical circuits off of your household's main service panel will not be nearly enough to supply a full-service auto workshop. Therefore, have a representative from your power company come out to your proposed site and determine the most advantageous means of supplying it with adequate electrical power. Chapter three will cover electricity in detail, but for now, realize that you may have to have a separate electrical panel installed just for your shop. Although the initial cost for separate electrical service may be high, the overall benefits will generally prove most worthwhile.

Heating an auto workshop can be accomplished in a variety of ways. Your primary concern should be what type of activities you will pursue in your shop. Do you plan on conducting a lot of painting sessions or other procedures that will require the use of flammable liquids? If so, you must realize that an open fire in a wood stove is absolutely out of the question during those times. Although natural gas and propane heaters require open flames, they can be completely shut down during painting and when using other flammable liquids. How practical would this be for you?

Along with electrical service, chapter three will cover more on shop heating systems. For now, though, be sure to note that some source of workshop heat should be identified and eventually described on your building plans.

The enjoyment of working on your special car inside a toasty workshop during a cold and rainy day could be rudely interrupted should your shirt sleeve dip into a puddle of cold water that had slipped in under a bay door while you were on a creeper changing the oil. Likewise, it is quite dangerous to use an electric power tool while standing in a shallow pool of water that has found its way into your shop through an opening under a small entry door.

Directing water runoff away from structures is a very important consideration. Water allowed to stagnate next to foundations has been known to cause mildew and moisture problems on the interior of structure walls. In addition, moisture can destroy wood framing and siding through a dry rot process. Water that flows freely into workshops is not only annoying but can be downright dangerous when it comes close to any source of electricity. Smooth concrete floors are as slippery as ice when they get wet—a true hazard for anyone, especially someone carrying a heavy tool or auto part.

Rainwater on shop roofs should be channeled through eaves-mounted gutters and then diverted from downspouts into *french drains*. This system of drainage incorporates perforated 3in or 4in plastic pipe buried in trenches around foundations. Trench bottoms and foundation sides should be covered with plastic to prevent water from escaping toward those directions. Pipe is placed in trenches at a downward angle to ensure that water runs toward a main drain, culvert, or other suitable water runoff area. Pipe and trenches are then filled with pea gravel to within a few inches of the ground surface.

Rain gutter downspouts should be routed so they dump roof water runoff into pipe sections that connect directly to french drain pipes. Surface water that

Rainwater runoff is a very important factor in almost every building construction project. Water allowed to stagnate next to wood walls will eventually cause dry rot problems, along with mildew, mold, and a host of other troubles. One way to help channel water away from structures is to install

eaves-mounted rain gutters with downspouts connected directly to drain pipes that route water to main sewer drains, natural runoff creeks, and other such systems. Be certain that pipes run downhill when installed to avoid problems with stagnate water pools underground.

filters through pea gravel and into pipe perforations will eventually flow out with rain gutter water to a desired runoff area. Other types of foundation drains utilize solid plastic pipe to capture rain gutter water and divert it quickly to a main drain. Building departments in regions which experience heavy seasonal rainfalls most assuredly will have information regarding the specific foundation drainage system preferred.

Driveway slope must also account for rainwater runoff. If your building site has a natural slope directly down the driveway toward your shop, you will have to install drains that can capture water before it reaches shop doors. Drains designed to be inserted into concrete or asphalt driveways are commonly available at lumber yards, hardware stores, and home improvement centers.

You should consider the effect loud noises emanating from your shop may have on family members and neighbors. If your shop is located close to residential structures, you may want to consider installing soundproofing material on shop walls. Although insulation and drywall will help to muffle some sounds, extra loud operations may require sound board additions to adequately abate loud pounding, air ratchet, air chisel, grinder, and other noises. Sound boards are available through most lumber yards.

Mention "creature comforts" to almost anyone with a full-sized auto workshop and you will be surprised at the number mentioned. Some of the most common are coffee pots, telephones, intercoms, large sinks with hot water, sound systems, comfortable chairs, and refrigerators. From there, enthusiasts have delighted themselves by installing bathrooms, microwave ovens, and television sets. For all intents and purposes, you can put anything in your shop you want.

Bathroom installations require plenty of thought prior to shop construction. Along with a water supply, toilets must have a large discharge pipe that connects directly to a sewer pipe or septic system. In most cases, building codes do not allow this pipe to go through footings or foundations. Therefore, when sewer pipes are located away from shop sites, toilet discharge pipes must either run under footings or down walls to the foundation and out from there. In regions where freezing winters are common, pipes cannot be run along the exterior of walls and must be routed completely under footings and foundations below frost lines to underground sewer pipes or septic systems.

Along with the routing of underground pipes, you have to be certain where you want to locate toilets and other bathroom fixtures so that initial plumbing inlets and outlets can be properly secured before concrete footings, foundations, and slab floors are poured. You can't have a toilet mount and water lines sticking up out of a floor in one spot and then decide to move it all after concrete has been poured and fin-

Driveway drains prevent rainwater runoff from entering garage or workshop areas from driveways that slope down toward structures. It is imperative that concrete be formed, poured, and shaped in such a way that slab surfaces slope toward drain openings. This new concrete slab was poured flat except for the last few, lighter-colored feet, which were angled toward the drain. A subsequent driveway will run toward the same drain but with an opposite slope, so that the drain will be located at the lowest low spot between the driveway and garage/shop.

ished. You will have to live with the original design or work very hard with a jackhammer to break out concrete in order to relocate those pipes.

Workshop bathrooms are most convenient, of course, while a shower may at first appear to be quite a luxury. However, this amenity might come in quite handy for those enthusiasts who plan to conduct a wide range of ongoing auto restoration activities which, in turn, could easily result in their getting plenty dirty and greasy. Sinks, on the other hand, could play a significant safety role in any workshop environment by providing a place where harmful substances can be thoroughly flushed from hands, arms, and faces with plenty of fresh water. Mirrors above sinks are very valuable for finding debris that has gotten into eyes, and for checking faces and heads for deposits of crud after working on undercarriages.

An auto workshop's size and its owner's budget will generally determine the types and amount of creature comforts included in any shop design. However, no matter how small the shop or limited the budget, make every attempt to provide your facility with a a telephone and a sink with running water. A sink is great for washing some auto parts, and most viable for flushing eyes and body parts subjected to corrosive liquids. A telephone could be a lifesaver when you find yourself all alone and in need of emergency services like medical aid or a fire engine. Along with that, a shop telephone comes in handy when you need to chase down parts and are much too dirty to be allowed entry into your home. Ron Weglin recommends a cordless telephone so you can actually look at vehicle assemblies while talking to vendors to ensure that parts being ordered will match old ones being replaced.

CHAPTER 3

ELECTRICAL AND HEATING SUPPLIES

With minimal guidance and support, almost anyone can learn how to accurately saw boards, pound nails, and hang drywall. Should the worst happen and a board get cut too short, one just has to go out and buy another. Bend a nail and you simply pull it out and use a replacement. Misjudge the cut on a piece of drywall and it might fit somewhere else. Small mistakes made during construction activities like these are easy to correct without any long-lasting or catastrophic results. When it comes to electricity and heating units, however, any number of errors could cause either serious damage to the system being worked on, a fire in the building receiving the service, or, worse yet, serious injury or death.

Electricity is a fascinating power source that is difficult to describe. Although it is virtually invisible, its power is likened to that of water forced through a hose. Water can flow a lot of volume through a big hose with little pressure, or a lot of pressure in a small hose with little volume, or a lot of volume and pressure through a large hose. Same with electricity—a small wire can give you a tremendous shock, as can a larger wire, depending upon the voltage and amperage flowing through.

NEVER work with electrical wires unless you are absolutely certain all power to them has been turned off. This goes for electrical outlets and light switches, too. In fact, if you do not have any experience working with electricity, save all electrical work for certified electricians.

The same advice goes for heating systems. Natural gas and propane piping must undergo an air pressure time test before being connected to a fuel source. Should a pipe joint or connection be loose or faulty, gas could escape and trigger an explosion or fire. Electrically operated heating systems present the same kinds of shock and shorting hazards as electrical wiring systems. In addition, electrical heaters feature coils that get extremely hot. These could cause fires when combustibles are placed too close. Incorrectly wired thermostats, could allow heating elements to continually heat up without turning off.

This electric, ceiling-mounted space heater does an outstanding job of quickly raising a workshop's temperature to a comfortable level. It runs off of 220V power and must be connected to the shop's electrical service panel perfectly. Incorrect wiring could cause a fire, small electrical explosion, complete disintegration of the heating unit, or electrocution of the installer. On the other hand, physical mounting of such a heater to the ceiling requires only minimal skills, like locating joists and inserting large lag bolts into them to support heater brackets.

In a nutshell, hire an electrician to properly install and connect your shop's electrical panel, wiring, and service outlets. Then, have a certified technician install and provide power to your shop's heating system.

The installation of natural gas, ceiling-mounted space heaters must be regarded with the same caution afforded electrically operated heaters. Although their fans generally only require common 110V power, pipe connections must be sealed completely to prevent any hint of a natural gas leak. Professional plumbers and natural gas appliance installers are required to pressure-test natural gas piping systems before they can be actually connected to gas meter supplies. Any leak in this system creates a potential for disaster, as escaping natural gas can accumulate in low-lying pockets and then explode with great force if it comes in contact with an ignition source.

Basic Electrical Considerations

Only so much water can be forced through a garden hose before it bursts. Likewise, only so much electricity can be forced through a wire before it gets hot, shorts out, and starts a fire. *Circuit breakers* are devices which serve to restrict the amount of electricity that can be drawn through wires. A circuit is simply defined as a wire which serves one large device, like an electric stove, or a series of small devices, like common wall outlets. Now, if a stove part should malfunction and cause the unit to draw more current than its circuit is designed for, a circuit breaker will automatically trip and turn off all electricity to it. The same goes for a series of small outlets when too many high-energy appliances are plugged in and operated at the same time.

This philosophy works for older fuse boxes, too. The difference is in the current controlling device: fuse versus circuit breaker. Where a circuit breaker will trip to its "off" position, much like a light switch, a fuse's element will physically burn through, thus breaking the electrical circuit. Once the above-normal draw of current is eliminated, a new fuse must replace the old one.

In addition to circuit breakers or fuses you should plan to install a ground fault circuit interrupter (GFCI) for each circuit. GFCIs look like normal wall outlets but are outfitted with "test" and "reset" buttons. Commonly found in newer bathrooms, GFCIs operate just like circuit breakers except much faster and in response to smaller electrical line variances.

Circuit breakers and fuses are rated on the basis of how many amperes (amps) of electricity they will allow to pass through a circuit before tripping or burning out. Generally, household circuits that provide power to wall outlets and light switches are confined to 15amp and 20amp circuit breakers. Larger breakers of 30, 40, 50, or 60amp ratings are used primarily for single heavy-use items, like electric water heaters, forced air furnaces, stoves, and clothes dryers. Because these individual units draw such large amounts of current, they are served by their own individual circuit breaker or fuse.

Electrical codes generally allow a combination of eight to ten common household outlets and light switches on a single 15amp circuit. Up to thirteen may be allowed for 20amp circuits. Remember, these are common household outlets that are designed to serve lamp and light fixtures, radios, television sets, and other small appliances. Without a doubt, you will constantly trip breakers or blow fuses if you try to operate two or more heavy-current-use power tools and/or equipment units at the same time from one small circuit.

Houses built more than forty years ago were commonly outfitted with 50amp or 60amp service at their fuse boxes. Today, because of the many electrical appliances at our disposal, new homes are frequently built with 200amp service panels. This means that a combination of 15, 20, 30, and up to 60amp circuit breakers can be connected and used off of a main panel, as long as the total capacity of all circuit breakers does not exceed 200amps.

Mike Holiman realized that he would need plenty of electrical current to supply welders, a heavy-duty air compressor, a host of power tools, and other power equipment. Because he wanted his shop to have plenty of power, he had the power company run a 400amp service to his workshop.

An incandescent light fixture was removed from this round electrical box and replaced with a common electrical outlet into which a fluorescent light is now plugged. Although the actual power supply and intent of this alteration is fine, installing a rectangular outlet inside a round box is not. Large gaps on each side of this outlet open into the area where portions of bare wires are exposed. Should a mop handle, piece of metal trim, or other item accidentally enter the opening, the outlet could short out causing a fire, or electrocuting the person holding the object. When incandescent lights are removed for the installation of regular outlets, their boxes must be replaced with those designed for outlets. Electrical supply components and the appliances they serve must always be installed and connected in accordance with standard electrical codes.

This is what the inside of a typical 200amp electrical service panel looks like. Three large wires coming in from the top are the main service lines from the power company supplies; power company installers normally provide this service for specific fees. The two large bare wires on the right are grounds, with the one on top coming from the main outside service and the other generally securely attached to a water line or long grounding rod pounded a few feet into the earth. Power brought to the service panel is transferred through circuit breakers to outlets and light switches. Plan to have a qualified electrician put such a panel in service for you to ensure its safe and efficient operation.

Each 220V appliance, like a welder or the air compressor, is served by its own separate circuit breaker. Various rows of lights run on their own circuits, and each wall's outlets are served by its own breaker. This means that Holiman and some friends could each operate a heavy-duty power tool all at the same time—as long as each 110V tool was plugged into an outlet on a separate wall. To be sure, this electrical setup is heavy-duty, but Holiman has never had a problem with breakers tripping.

Along with electrical service and circuit breaker loads, you have to be sure to install wiring that is heavy enough to handle the current loads. First off, *always* use copper wire in lieu of aluminum. In the past, houses with aluminum wiring experienced problems with wire ends loosening up at its connections. This results in unexpected arcing that creates fire hazards. Exceptions are extra large aluminum wire bundles used to service main breaker and distribution panels. For service to outlets and switches

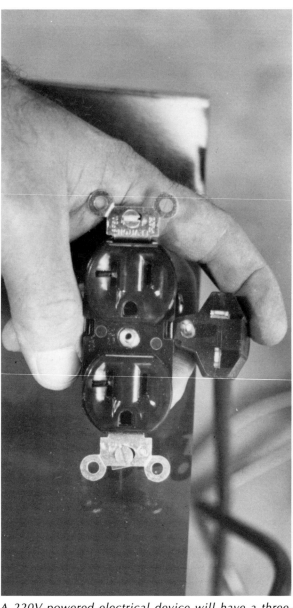

A 220V-powered electrical device will have a three-pronged plug designed with one flat prong installed at an angle opposite of the others'. This will plug into a special outlet. To ensure the uninterrupted and safe operation of 220V compressors and other heavy electrical-use equipment, dedicate one circuit and circuit breaker to each such unit.

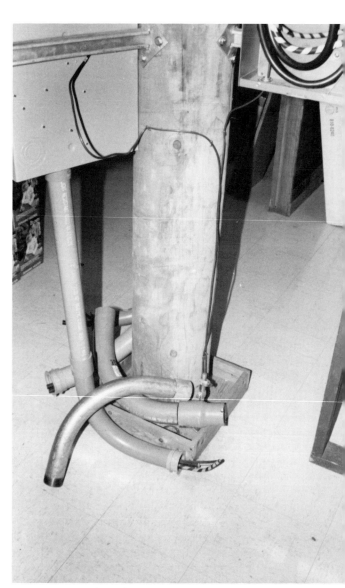

Large sections of conduit (pipe) are attached to electrical service panels and serve as protection for main electric service lines that run from utility poles or underground electrical vaults to panels. You will see them as roof corner goose-necks that receive power from utility pole lines, or at the bottom of panels served by underground vaults. Ask your electrician to install large conduit so that additional power supply lines can easily be brought to your shop for a future 400amp panel as your automotive tasks increase.

from your shop's main electrical panel out through walls or in the attic, use copper wire.

The copper wire size required for various circuits is determined by the electrical loads that will pass through. For example, number-18 wire is very small and commonly used for lamp cords. Number-3 wire is very large and used for commercial and industrial applications. To give an example for an auto workshop: A garage door opener should be protected by a 20amp circuit breaker and served with a number-12 copper wire.

The calculations required to arrive at specific levels of amp service and the size of wires needed for various applications can be quite complicated. Along with the current needed to serve combinations of lights, tools, and equipment, voltage drops and the length of service wires are factors that must be included. There is a lot more to it than just that, and you are earnestly encouraged to seek the assistance of a qualified electrical contractor when planning and installing the electrical service and wiring layout for your workshop.

Electrical Cost Considerations

Don't be surprised if you hiccup the first time an electrical contractor gives you a cost estimate for complete installation of an electrical system in your workshop. Right off the bat, getting a 200amp or 400amp service to your building will be expensive. The service panel box and breakers might also throw your budget into a spasm. Then there are wiring, boxes, outlets, switches, and cover plates. And don't forget the contractor's labor fees.

To help defray this overall cost, learn exactly which type of service panel box is needed and what size wire is required. Then, go to garage sales and swap meets in an attempt to find these items. Independent electricians retire and move out of areas, and will frequently sell their accumulated treasures at tremendous discounts. You should also talk with the managers of hardware stores and home improvement centers to see if they have any surplus lengths of wire that could be bought for significant discounts.

Plastic electrical outlet and switch boxes sell for as little as five for a dollar, and lots of home improvement centers offer outlets and switches for less than a dollar each. Be sure to read the fine print on the back of outlets to be certain they are designed for the current rating of the circuit breakers they will be connected to. Cover plates are very inexpensive, so plan on buying them new, too.

Shop around, look for sales, and get estimates from more than one electrical contractor. While talking to contractors, find out how much of the labor you can provide by drilling holes in studs and pulling wire yourself. After all, those tasks are easy, and what you really want from an electrical contractor is his or her expertise in hooking up everything safely, reliably, and according to code. You might also check

your Christmas card list to see if you have a relative or friend who is a certified electrician and might be interested in trading labor—his or her electrical work for your auto body, repair, or tune-up labor.

Electrical Outlet Locations

Electrical service panels cannot be installed until a shop structure is completely framed. The building department may require that the structure be roofed and sided first, or you may decide to wait until these items are in place to protect panels from unexpected rain showers. Once a panel is installed, holes are systematically drilled through studs and top plates so electrical wiring can be fed through them and brought out where outlets, lights, and switch boxes have been installed. With all electricity turned off at

Electrical conduit is normally sold in 10ft lengths. An assortment of inside-diameter sizes is available at electric supply stores and many lumber yards. Ron Weglin suggests auto workshops be outfitted with large conduit lines mounted to finished wall surfaces—as opposed to standard, inner wall installations. He believes that additional electrical power can most easily be installed through accessible, large diameter conduit capable of accepting more wires, rather than through opening walls to make wire connections and install junction boxes. This is a valid point, especially for those who plan to construct small workshops now and add onto them at later dates.

the main breaker, of course, outlets and switches are then connected. Cover plates are not installed until after drywall has been hung.

Outlet and switch boxes are nailed to studs at desired locations. To ensure they will stick out far enough to fit flush with layers of drywall, use a small piece of drywall of the appropriate thickness as a guide (remember, 5/8in drywall on walls that divide shop and living areas and on all ceilings; 1/2in or 5/8in drywall for other walls). Simply hold a small piece of drywall flush with the face of a stud, and position the outlet box up to the drywall's front side. This way, assuming the outlet hole is correctly cut, a box's front edge will reach out to the front side of drywall and allow outlet or light switch ears to firmly rest against the drywall face for a tight fit.

An electrical outlet located behind and below a workbench is of little use, unless you like to crawl around on your hands and knees while straining to

One electrical outlet with only two receptacles limits the number of items that can be used at any one time. This can be a problem around workbenches when cordless tools need their batteries recharged and one wants to use other electric power tools at the same time. For those instances when current to more than two electrically powered items is needed, the convenience of double outlets with four receptacles is really appreciated. The cost to outfit workshops with double outlet boxes is very small compared to the convenience and efficiency they offer. Consider wiring each outlet to different circuits in order to avoid overloading individual circuits when all four receptacles are used at the same time.

Electrical outlets should be located for maximum convenience. In auto workshops, outlets placed a foot or two off of the floor are generally useless, as they will be blocked by workbenches, cabinets, and equipment. Plan to install workshop electrical outlets at waist or chest heights to best accommodate service needs. As you can see in this photo, the chest-high electrical outlet that serves this drill press and grinder is much more convenient than one located close to the floor.

reach it. Much more convenient locations for auto workshop electrical wall outlets are at waist or chest heights, or just above workbenches. Ceiling outlets can be very convenient as well.

Before installing wires and outlet boxes, draw a floor plan envisioning the positions of workbenches, welding booths, an air compressor, and so on. Then, try to visualize what type of work will be conducted at various locations inside the shop. On your drawing, note where different types of electrical power will be needed. Plan to install your welder's outlet at the site where most welding will take place. Do likewise for the air compressor, plasma cutter, and other 220V equipment.

Since lots of power tool work may be done at a specific workbench, you might consider installing two or three double outlets (four plug) a foot or so above the bench top. Plan to serve each outlet with a different circuit breaker so that more than one tool can be used at one time without the worry of breakers tripping.

Electrical outlets can go anywhere you want them. The trick is deciding just what equipment is going to be used where. An outlet by a telephone would be nice, especially if you want to hook up an answering machine. Where will a coffee pot go? How about a shop vacuum? Drill press? Lathe? Bench grinder? Sound system? Refrigerator? Microwave oven? Computer? Portable lights? Diagnostic equipment? Television? Upholstery sewing machine? Glue gun? Battery charger? And so on.

Ceiling-mounted electrical outlets may seem extravagant until you decide upon the installation of an extension cord reel. The same is true for power garage door openers. And don't forget a couple of weatherproof outlets on the outside of your shop to supply a power washer and a wet/dry vacuum. It doesn't take long to total up quite a few electrical outlets, does it?

Now what about light switches? The most convenient spot for switches that operate ceiling lights is right next to entry doors. This allows you to flip on lights as soon as you enter the shop. It also enables you to turn them off as you exit the building, as opposed to groping around in the dark until you find a door.

Auto workshops can almost never have too many lights. For that reason, plan to install a few rows of fluorescent ceiling lights, with each row wired to a separate switch. This way, you can turn on just one row for minimal illumination, two for greater light, and so on. More about lights in the next chapter, but for now, seriously consider which switch locations would be most advantageous.

Welders and Plasma Cutters

Older welders almost always required a 220V service because most welding was done on thick chunks of metal. Nowadays, body skins are very thin and only require small welding currents for patching

panels and other work. To that end, a number of companies have developed smaller welding machines that operate on 110V household currents.

Although these smaller welders are capable of sustaining welds while plugged into a 110V outlet, they still require a lot of current. Most welder guidelines recommend that tools have an individual, dedicated outlet served by a single 30amp circuit breaker.

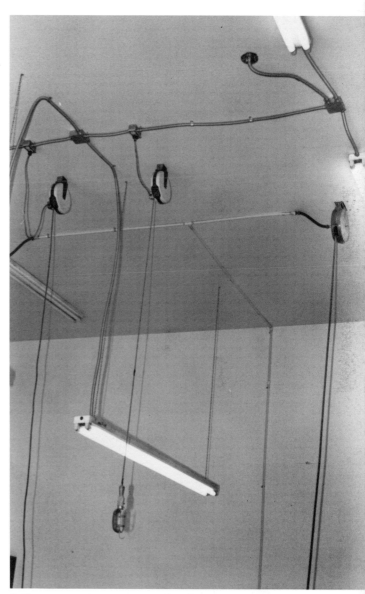

Ceiling-mounted extension cord reels are very convenient accessories. Their out-of-the-way location keeps them from getting tangled up with other shop items scattered about the floor. Regular-use, heavy-duty 110V extension cord reels can be outfitted with droplights and outlets for use in engine compartments and other dimly lit spaces. Extra-heavy-duty cord reels might also be considered for high-electrical-use equipment needed in different shop areas at any given time, like power washers, mobile air compressors, welders, and the like.

This ensures that machines are safely fed adequate amounts of current and not hindered by the operation of anything else on a circuit. In other words, a single number-10 or number-12 wire should run directly from a 30amp circuit breaker to a single outlet.

Larger welders requiring a 220V service must also be fed electricity through their own separate circuit breakers. Because these machines will draw heavy amounts of electrical current, they are generally equipped with special 220V plugs that can only be inserted into matching outlets. Electrical clothes dryers have these large plugs which feature three prominent, big-bladed prongs.

Plasma cutters use electricity and clean air to burn out and blow away metal. They cut quickly and very cleanly. Like welders, a plasma cutter requires a 220V service and is outfitted with a special plug that requires a matching outlet. As with any other piece of 220V equipment, a plasma cutter should be served by a separate circuit breaker, wire, and outlet.

Workshop Heating

Already briefly mentioned were the hazards associated with open-flame wood stoves and space heaters and the simultaneous use of paint products and other flammable liquids. These simply do not

With the advent of thinner autobody skins came a need for welders with power ranges low enough to produce effective welds without burning through panel material. Hence, the introduction of wire feed welders capable of operating off of standard 110V household electrical circuits. Although many 110V welders like this one come from manufacturers with regular three-pronged plugs that can be inserted into normal outlets, manufacturers recommend these units be served with separate 30amp circuits and circuit breakers dedicated only to their use. Therefore, as you plan for individual 220V circuits for heavy-use equipment, also make plans for separate 110V circuits to serve welders and other high-amperage appliances.

This HTP plasma cutter does an outstanding job of cutting metal quickly and accurately without leaving behind exaggerated jagged edges or slag. Because a great deal of electrical power is needed for its efficient operation, a heavy-duty electrical plug and outlet are required, along with a dedicated 220V circuit and circuit breaker. Your auto workshop floor plan should indicate a specific area where special equipment like this will be used so that sufficient electrical power and designated outlets can be conveniently and safely installed during shop construction and initial setup.

mix. Therefore, if your shop will be a place where many flammable liquids will be frequently in use, plan to look around for a heating system that can be completely shut down during flammable liquid work, or one that offers a combustion chamber located outdoors.

If you won't often use paint products and flammable liquids or do a lot of work on fuel systems, then a wood stove is a relatively inexpensive means of heating your shop. This is especially true for areas where firewood is cheap. Wood stoves can be bought new at stores or used at swap meets, garage sales, and flea markets. Some ambitious auto enthusiasts with lots of metalworking and welding experience might even build their own.

Wood stoves do have a few drawbacks in exchange for their relative low cost to purchase and operate. They cannot heat areas very quickly, and accurately maintaining specific shop temperatures is difficult and time consuming. It seems the stoves either get too hot or not nearly hot enough. Wood stoves take time to get used to, and you must practice adjusting dampeners and stoking fires in order to comfortably maintain a given shop temperature.

Electric baseboard heat is very expensive to operate, especially in winter climates where snow and freezing temperatures are daily encounters. These units are rather inexpensive to purchase, but you may need more than one to properly heat your shop. On the up side, they can be turned on to warm a shop and then shut down during painting or fuel system repairs.

Electrically powered space heaters are much more efficient than base board heaters for workshop heating. Their powerful fans force hot air out into shop areas to heat them in just a few minutes. As with other electric heaters, they may be turned off any time flammable liquids are in use. They are not cheap, but will quickly pay for themselves in convenience and user comfort.

Far less expensive to operate than electric space heaters, natural gas and propane models do a magnificent job of initially heating workshops and then maintaining comfortable climates throughout the day.

Ceiling-mounted space heaters are very common sights in automotive workshops. Along with heating large open spaces quickly and efficiently, the units are frequently located in shop corners where they do not take up valuable working space. The 220V electric model in Mike Holiman's shop is wired through the attic, eliminating unsightly wires

or conduit nearby. The natural gas heater in Dan Mycon's autobody and paint shop receives its power and natural gas supply from conduit and pipe mounted to the wall. Both of these heaters can be completely shut down during operations that entail the use of flammable liquids, or that will result in extra dusty atmospheres, like autobody sanding.

61

Hot water heating systems can also employ ceiling-mounted units. Electrically operated fans are turned on by thermostat controls to push air over coils filled with hot water. Water is heated in a boiler and then forced through pipes by way of a pump. In addition to feeding ceiling fans, hot water pipes could be installed inside concrete floors to keep them warm and help radiate heat up from their surface. It is imperative that hot water systems be maintained according to manufacturer's instructions, especially with regard to antifreeze levels when pipes are subjected to freezing temperatures.

A wide variety of heaters is available through heating appliance stores, electric supply houses, and many home improvement centers. It is important to study each different model to understand its capabilities and limitations. In addition, you should be aware that baseboard and wall-mounted heaters require open space around them, a situation which will cut down available workshop wall space.

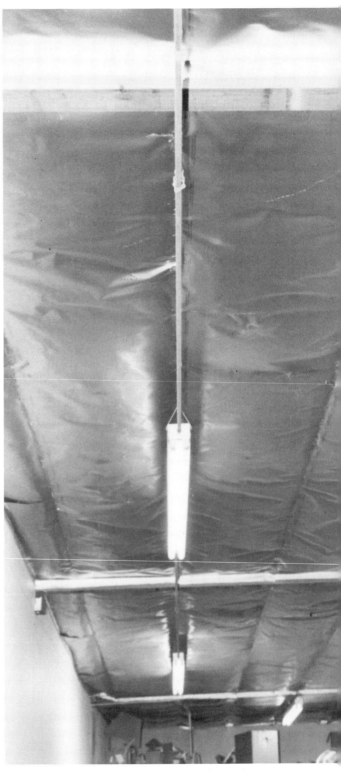

In order to help the space heaters in his shop achieve maximum performance and economical operation, Mycon had a special type of reflective-backed insulation installed on his ceiling. The building which houses his shop has a flat roof that does not offer a large enough open space to accommodate extra-thick insulation. In addition to radiating heat back to the floor, this silver-colored material helps to reflect and disperse fluorescent light.

An ideal model to consider is one that *does not* employ a constant pilot light. Instead, it will have an igniter that lights a flame once its thermostat signals the heater to turn on. This feature allows you to simply turn a thermostat down to zero while conducting paint work, without fear of a pilot light or flame igniting flammable atmospheres.

Hot water heaters are another option. The most critical factor in their maintenance is to keep the appropriate level of antifreeze in the piping system. A few different hot water systems are available from most heating companies. Visit some heating appliance stores and learn about the various models and option packages. Check in the yellow pages under *Heating Equipment*.

Air Conditioning

For those workshops in regions where winter climates are mild but summers are terribly hot, an air conditioning system may be worth the investment. Rick and Ron Weglin, owners of Harrah's Automotive in Seattle, Washington, would give almost anything for air conditioning during those few weeks in summer when temperatures soar into the high nineties and they have to work under the hoods of sun-baked cars.

One would surmise that desert areas in Arizona and southern California would require air conditioning systems for auto workshops, as well as for every other building. Justifiable in some areas, though something of a luxury in others, air conditioning might be a shop option worth investigating. Be sure the unit you choose can cool a shop your size, and that return air ducts are equipped with heavy-duty filters that can handle the sanding dust and other air pollution created in your shop.

Regardless of the types of water heaters and space heaters installed in your automotive workshop, always make certain the appliances have plenty of open space around them to avoid potential fire hazards. Items stacked next to heating units like this are susceptible to combustion from pilot lights and heating elements. If at all possible, segregate such equipment in areas that will not be cluttered with combustible items.

CHAPTER 4

LIGHTING

Special equipment used for specific repair and restoration procedures should be outfitted with individual accessory lamps. Some pieces of equipment are fitted with stock lamps from their manufacturer, while others may be complemented with any of a wide assortment of clamp-type workbench or desk lamp models. The Smithy Company.

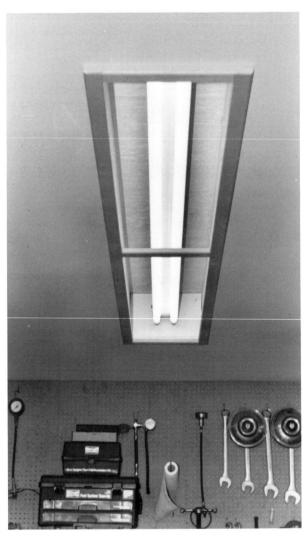

The ceiling in Garry Allen's Jags Plus automotive workshop is outfitted with recessed, 8ft, two-tube fluorescent light fixtures. These do an excellent job of illuminating his work space, and their recessed design makes them less vulnerable to damage than hanging lights. Wood moulding around light openings offers a finished appearance, and drywall installed around the recessed surfaces protects wood joists and other structural members from the lights' constant heat.

Excellent automotive workshop illumination should be a prime consideration for every work place, regardless of its size. Inadequate lighting will not only cause frustration during repair work, but it could conceal such hazardous conditions as engine blocks barely supported on motor mount edges, transmissions teetering on lifts, electrical boots improperly seated, coil spring compressors misaligned, and a host of other accidents just waiting to happen.

Groping around in the dark almost always leads to problems, from bumping shins against hard metal objects to banging foreheads into shelves. Main light switches should be conveniently located next to entrance/exit doors, and wired so that they can be operated at both a small entry door and a main bay door. In addition to general shop lighting, separate light fixtures should be installed for extra illumination over workbenches, buffing wheel stands, small parts and fastener storage areas, paint booths, pits, parts cleaning tubs, and the like. In a nutshell, automotive workshops can almost never be outfitted with too much light.

It would be ideal if shops could be lit up with as much candlepower as is provided by the sun. After all, sunlight is our most brilliant light source. However, as discussed earlier, the sun's ultraviolet rays can bring about problems like faded upholstery, paint oxidation, and premature material aging. So the object is to find, design, and implement a means of artificial lighting that will not cause damage to eyes or auto accessories yet be bright enough to accommodate all of your auto endeavors.

Overhead workshop (ceiling) lights are a given. Every shop has to have some, just like each has to have at least one garage (bay) door. But how many lights are needed and in which pattern should they be installed? Are fluorescent lights better than standard incandescent lights?

There doesn't seem to be any set lighting standard for all workshop designs. You can certainly outfit yours with whatever lights you deem most efficient and cost-effective, as long as the type of work undertaken is not compromised (made unsafe) in any way.

Lights and Safety

Flammable atmospheres of any kind require explosion-proof light fixtures designed especially for the type of hazardous operation conducted in the area illuminated. Many spray paint booths, for example, feature fluorescent lamps mounted on exterior walls sealed off from booth interiors by heavy plastic gasket-equipped panels. This design prevents flammable

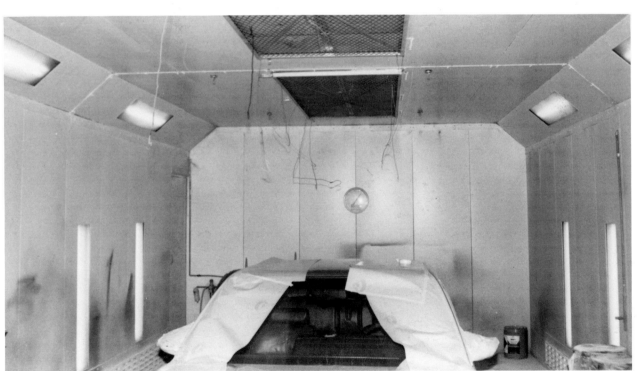

The spray paint booth inside Mycon's Newlook Autobody features a number of bright fluorescent light fixtures that are sealed off from the actual painting area by way of plastic panels and gaskets. Burned-out light tubes are replaced from outside the booth. This kind of lighting arrangement is designed to prevent flammable atmospheres from coming *in contact with potential electrical arc ignition sources inside light assemblies. Should you plan to pursue painting endeavors and other operations that involve flammable liquids, seriously consider installing explosion-proof light fixtures in hazardous work areas.*

paint sprays from coming in contact with electrical arcs or any ignition source within light fixtures. Those mounted inside paint booths are of a special explosion-proof design which encloses electrical components so that flammable vapors and potential ignition sources are completely separated.

In addition to spray paint booths, paint mixing rooms, parts washing solvent vats, sandblast cabinets, and other special process areas require safety light fixtures in order to eliminate electrical arcs igniting flammable vapors or dust clouds. Along with fire hazards, mixtures of flammable gases with ignition sources could cause violent explosions.

Safety lights are outfitted with *rough service* bulbs that withstand knocks and jolts much better than standard bulbs. These fixtures must be able to seal in such a way that their electrical supply and connections are completely separated from surrounding environments while heat generated by their bulbs is dissipated appropriately. Likewise, especially over solvent tubs, lights have to have sturdy lenses that will not crack or shatter when accidentally sprayed with a cool, yet flammable, solvent. Should you have a need for safety lights in your spray paint booth or other work area, locate sources for explosion-proof safety lights in the yellow pages under the headings of *Safety Equipment, Lighting Equipment,* or *Lighting Fixtures—Repairing and Maintenance.*

General Lighting Requirements

The majority of automotive workshops feature fluorescent lights on their ceilings. These units offer widely dispersed illumination patterns, especially when ceilings and walls are painted white. You can purchase 4ft or 8ft fluorescent fixtures that accommodate one, two, or four tubes each. Short units with one bulb might be fine under cabinets to illuminate small desks, but would be highly inefficient if suspended from ceilings. On the other hand, a 4ft unit with four light tubes might be great for lighting up workbench areas or small parts storage closets.

Large ceiling areas require a series of fluorescent light fixtures for optimum illumination. If your shop is divided into separate bays, consider wiring each row of lights to a separate switch. This way, you'll have the option of lighting up an entire shop for regular work activities or simply illuminating one or two areas for periods when work is confined to only those spaces.

The decision between 4ft and 8ft fixtures is one of convenience and ceiling space. Naturally, your shop's ceiling must have plenty of 8ft long slots to accommodate larger units, whereas 4ft models can be squeezed between other facilities, like skylights, open bay doors, heating systems, and so on. Another consideration is the storage and handling of 8ft light tubes. How easy will it be for you to change them? Will your shop offer a safe space for the storage of these long items?

Extra-large professional auto repair facilities are frequently outfitted with 8ft fluorescent lights simply because there is so much area to cover and each unit is capable of putting out a lot of light. Cost is another factor. Would it be cheaper for you to buy and install six 8ft lights, or nine 4ft models? Bulb cost is also something to check on—which will be most cost effective? Shop around at hardware stores and home

Many economical fluorescent light fixtures come with short cords designed for three-pronged electrical outlets. These units require ceiling-mounted outlets that are operated by switches closer to ground level. An extension cord/droplight reel can also be plugged into such outlets but will only work when the overhead lights are turned on. Note: This outlet should be fitted with a cover to prevent dust, insects, and other contaminants from entering the outlet box.

improvement centers to determine which are most economical.

Basically, design your shop's ceiling light capacity so that it will offer a minimum 3/4W of fluorescent light per square foot of shop space. A 30ft by 40ft shop (1200sq-ft), for example, would require fifteen 60W bulbs or twelve 80W units. You have to decide whether 4ft or 8ft fixtures will best fit your ceiling dimensions. For adequate lighting with incandescent bulbs, figure a minimum of 2W per square foot. For a 1200 square foot shop area, this will require twenty-four 100W lights.

From this comparison, you can see that fluorescent lights offer more illumination with fewer fixtures. Along with that, fluorescent tubes last about five to ten times longer than incandescent bulbs, and use almost one-third less electricity for equal amounts of light. In addition, the shadows commonly caused by crisp incandescent lights are virtually eliminated with fluorescent lighting.

Lights should be installed in a pattern that most evenly disperses illumination. There must be a degree of common sense in the design, as well. If your shop measures 24ft by 24ft (576 square feet—the size of a regular two-car garage) and you install four fluorescent light fixtures, each with two 4ft tubes, you would

Four-tube fluorescent lights offer a lot more illumination to specific areas than two-tube models. They are not usually needed on ceilings, where overall shop light should be widely dispersed by a number of separate two-tube fixtures evenly spaced overhead. Rather, four-tube units are most convenient next to specific workbench and table areas for maximum illumination where repair and restoration procedures are more confined and generally involve small parts.

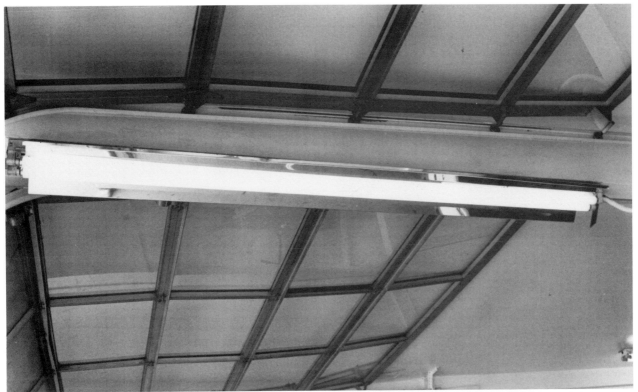

Even with bay doors open during daylight hours, most automotive workshops still require the extra illumination afforded by ceiling lights and other lamp fixtures. Therefore, realize that open bay/garage doors will block the light from fix-tures mounted to the ceiling above them. If this poses a problem in your garage or workshop, plan to install lights between doors, or add extra lights to both sides of single-door installations.

not want each fixture placed in a corner. This would leave the center of your work area almost completely unlit, especially when garage doors are up and cabinets or shelves extend close to the ceiling.

A more logical lighting plan for this medium-sized shop would locate fluorescent fixtures more centrally—maybe two units down the center of each stall, in line with the positions in which vehicles will park. Extra lights could then be installed over workbench areas.

For maximum illumination above this workbench where pinstriping and lettering paint is mixed, Roy Dunn installed a shelf outfitted with 4ft, four-tube, fluorescent lights. You can see in this photo that the area is lit up quite well, and the position of the fixtures is such that shadows are not cast on work areas when Dunn bends over them to get a closer look at whatever he is working on at the time. Consideration must be given to the material inside the light recesses to accommodate for heat generated by the tubes.

Larger shops will require more light fixtures. Space lights evenly apart so that each square foot of floor area is covered with equal light. Use 1/4in graph paper to draw your lighting design to scale. Two-bulb fluorescent light fixtures are generally about 8in wide. Those with four light tubes will be much wider. Bring a tape measure to a home improvement center and measure fixtures you plan to purchase in order to more accurately determine where they might be installed. This facet of your workshop construction project must be completed before actual electrical wires and boxes are installed. If not, your electrician will have to estimate their location.

Overhead lights mounted inside ceilings are preferred because they offer the most actual working light, do not hang down as targets for mop handles or other tall implements, and do not accumulate dust and cobwebs like suspended fixtures. This suggests another good reason for deciding early which light fixtures are planned for the shop: Their dimensions must be known so that light boxes can be accurately framed inside ceiling joists or roof rafters (in the case of cathedral ceilings). Although fluorescent bulbs do not get nearly as hot as incandescent bulbs, they generate heat nonetheless. For that reason, their framed ceiling boxes must be lined with drywall to prevent bulb-to-wood contact—a possible fire hazard.

Workbench Area Lighting

You must remember that ceiling light will not always accommodate the specific needs of intricate work areas like workbench tops. Rebuilding carburetors, soldering electrical components, and working on small auto parts requires lots of overall light in order to plainly see tiny screws, O-rings, wires, clips, and so on. Ideally, plan to install one or two 4ft, two- or four-bulb, fluorescent lights about 48in above workbench tops. This should offer you a great deal of bright working light.

If a cabinet or cupboard has been built above your workbench, install a small fluorescent fixture under its base to help illuminate workbench surface areas. This will compensate for shadows that may be caused by your head and shoulders as you lean over to get better views of auto parts. If need be, purchase an inexpensive long-arm desk lamp that is adjustable in a number of different directions. These units are portable and easily mounted to workbench lips by way of simple screw and base assemblies. Use a drop light when additional illumination is needed during work with extra small auto parts, components, or assemblies.

Drop Light Location

Almost any in-depth repair or maintenance attempted under the hood of a vehicle will require a drop light, especially if that vehicle is parked inside an auto workshop. Even though you can always stretch an extension cord and drop a light from an electrical wall outlet, wouldn't it be much more convenient to have a drop light attached to a cord reel mounted to the ceiling? For that matter, what about two or three combination extension-cord-and-drop-light reels located at different sites around the shop?

Without a doubt, one of these units should be located close to each area where engine compartments are destined to be worked on. Install one unit at the front and directly between each bay of a two-stall workshop so that it can be used under the hoods of cars parked in either stall. A second reel may be most useful centered between the outer portion of a parking stall and a nearby workbench. Ceiling-mounted drop light/extension cord reels at each corner of every parking stall might appear to be a bit too much, until you find yourself working on an undercarriage and in need of two or three times more light than is available from just one unit.

Cord reels are just about useless when mounted in the center of a parking stall, unless that area is wide open and cars are parked elsewhere. All ceiling-mounted electrical, air, and water hose reels should be installed between bays and close to forward shop areas. This not only facilitates access, but is also most convenient because the majority will be needed in or around engine compartments. With that in mind, be sure reel cords or hoses are sufficiently long to reach all corners of each parking stall they serve. This is especially true for air hoses that may be required to

reach all four tires on a full-length pickup truck or older American classic.

For those ambitious enthusiasts who frequently find themselves working on family or friends' cars parked just outside their overflowing shop space, consider a ceiling-mounted drop light/extension cord unit placed just inside a bay door. This option serves the rear of parking stalls as well as providing for those unexpected repairs on crippled autos parked just outside.

Standard drop lights which incorporate an incandescent bulb protected by a metal housing and cage must be handled carefully. Be aware that housings may get hot enough to burn your skin should they come into direct contact. Likewise, a hot drop light shield could burn or melt plastic, vinyl, and similar

Combination extension cord/droplights are exceptionally handy workshop accessories. They should be located near the front of shops where most under-the-hood operations take place. Reels are designed to hold cords stable at certain lengths by way of ratchet mechanisms. Users can pull out as much cord as needed, lock the spring-loaded return assembly, and use cords and lights without placing any unnecessary tension on them. Droplights are easy to stabilize under hoods, and their extension cord outlets provide immediate power for electric tools without the hassle of stringing out regular extension cords over workshop floors.

Portable desk lamps with long, articulating arms are great workbench accessories. They are especially useful while working to assemble or adjust small auto parts and components where extra light is needed to illuminate small openings, fine print, and other tiny items. Lamps like this are frequently sold at home improvement centers and discount stores for under $10.

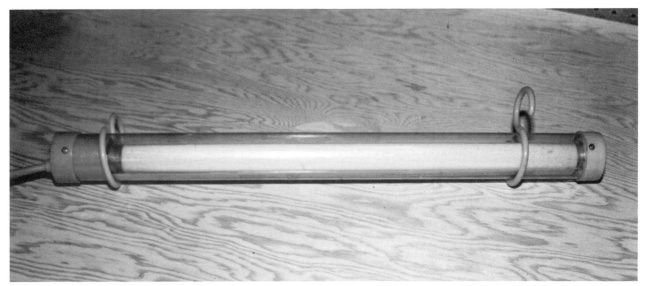

The light metal housings on standard droplights tend to get quite hot from the heat radiated by their incandescent light bulbs. This poses a problem with their use in confined spaces, in that they cannot be set on top of or next to materials that could melt or catch fire. Therefore, consider using fluorescent droplights in tight places to avoid such dilemmas. Units like this offer lots of light without the concern of extra-hot housings coming in contact with vulnerable materials.

Illuminating areas under raised vehicles is most frequently accomplished with droplights. This could be enhanced with fluorescent lights mounted low on side walls next to work stalls. Bill Snyder uses these wall-mounted lights to brighten autobody repair operations conducted on the sides of vehicles. They also do a good job of dispersing light under those cars and trucks raised off of the floor with jack stands. Wall-mounted lights, used in conjunction with floor lamps or droplights, generally offer sufficient illumination for most undercarriage repair and restoration.

soft materials. For those reasons, be certain drop lights are suspended from metallic surfaces by their hooks.

Fluorescent drop lights are larger than standard drop lights but do not get nearly as hot. In fact, most of these designs barely get warm to the touch. So if you need a drop light to illuminate engine compartment caverns where access is extra tight, consider fluorescent drop lights in lieu of incandescent lights.

Under-vehicle Illumination

Vehicle undercarriages are some of the toughest areas to light up. A drop light may be sufficient for concentrated spots, but what if an entire front section needs light for Concours-quality cleaning? Auto body expert Bill Snyder suggests using a household halogen outdoor light fixture.

Halogen light bulbs are very powerful. Some single units are capable of brightly illuminating entire yards. Can you imagine how well they could light up a vehicle's undercarriage or wheelwell? Snyder purchased a single halogen yard light fixture for under $8 at a home center. Though the light was designed for installation onto an electrical box, Snyder mounted his on top of a piece of metal conduit using the box's fittings. That piece of conduit was slid inside a larger pipe so it had a vertical moving range from about 3ft to a little over 5ft. A screw was threaded into a collar at the top of the larger pipe and is used to secure the smaller pipe at its adjusted height. A base for the stand was made from pieces of scrap metal.

In addition to this light, Snyder mounted an electrical outlet box onto the stand's larger pipe. The unit has four outlets and doubles as a handy rack for an extension cord. Now, whenever Snyder needs light *and* an electrical source, both are quickly available from just this device. The stand works great for lighting undercarriages on vehicles raised with a lift. It is easily focused on particular areas when adjusted to an optimum height. Since the light fixture itself can swivel up and down, it is also well-suited for illuminating engine compartments.

After he made this stand, Snyder realized that a much shorter unit was needed for work he does under cars and trucks that are simply supported by jack stands. He bought another $8 halogen yard light, a few electrical box fittings, and a short piece of conduit. Some scrap metal pieces were located for a base, and in just a half hour or so, he had a very handy, bright, and portable undercarriage and wheelwell light. About the only complaint he has relates to the lamp brightness. If a light is placed at the front of an undercarriage and aimed toward the back, and Snyder crawls under the car from the back and faces forward, the bright light shining toward his face is almost blinding. He suggests that bright halogen lights be placed behind users so that both light beams and eyes are focused toward the same direction.

Halogen light bulbs are quite expensive. At some stores, replacement bulbs alone cost almost as much as an entire yard light fixture complete with bulbs. These bulbs are also very sensitive while lit. Therefore, be keenly aware of their location and try to avoid knocking them over or smacking them with a hand tool or other implement. Additionally, halogens

This is a handy, multipurpose, portable light built by Bill Snyder. It combines a 4ft, two-tube, fluorescent light with an outdoor halogen lamp and a four-receptacle electrical outlet complete with an extra-long service cord. An old auto wheel is used as a base that supports a pipe welded to it. Considering that an old wheel and section of pipe are available for next to nothing, a portable light like this should cost less than $25 to construct.

must be handled carefully when changed. Never touch a halogen with your bare hand; oil from your skin will cause hot spots on the bulb which will cause it to burn out prematurely. Halogen lights also get *extremely* hot, even hotter than incandescent drop light bulbs and housings. Because of this, you must be cautious in their placement, especially under cars, where they could easily come in contact with low-lying brake lines, fuel lines, painted surfaces, mud flaps, radiator hoses, loosened belts, and the like.

WARNING—never place any drop light too close to fuel lines or fuel tank connections being worked on, nor close to a section of fuel line that suffers a leak. In far too many cases, drops of cool or cold fuel (gasoline) have fallen on hot light bulbs, causing them to immediately shatter and, in turn, causing light filaments to arc. These electrical arcs have served as explosive ignition sources for fuel leaking from loosened connections or broken lines, starting fires that have engulfed mechanics, automobiles, workshops, garages, and attached or nearby homes.

Light Fixture Styles and Cost

Those auto enthusiasts who cherish any restoration or repair activity generally derive a great deal of pleasure from locating sought-after classic auto parts at swap meets or garage sales. This excitement is accentuated when a real bargain is made, and the purchase more resembles theft than an equitable sales transaction. In other words, they really enjoy buying good stuff at super cheap prices, even if parts need rebuilding or restoring before they are usable.

Their philosophy is simple: why pay through the nose for a new part, when a used one can be found for a fraction of the cost, and restoration will cost next to nothing? Save money for more parts, right? This theory holds true for many shop accessories, too.

By all means, go to hardware stores and home improvement centers to see what kinds of light fixtures are available and what they cost. By shopping around, you will get a very good idea of how you want to set up the lighting system for your shop. Check with fellow car club members and other enthusiasts to find out which types of light fixtures have worked best for them. Do they like 4ft fluorescent lights, or longer 8ft models? Do multiple bulb incandescent fixtures work best for certain restoration operations, and halogen bulbs for others? Do they have experience altering older, suspension-type fluorescent lights into ceiling-mounted styles? The bottom line is to figure out which light styles will work best for you and the activities you have planned for your shop. Once you have selected the size and type of lights you want for your work space, start shopping around for the best buys.

Prices for brand new, 4ft, double-tube fluorescent lights start at around $8. These are economy fixtures designed to hang from ceilings by short chains, and

are equipped with short, pigtail cords and three-prong plugs. You will have to suspend them right next to an electrical outlet, outfit them with an extension cord, or rewire them with a new cord long enough to reach a nearby outlet. A step up from economy lights are similar models with better frames and longer cords, available for around $30. The more bells and whistles, the more you'll have to pay. If you want fluorescent light assemblies complete with all mounting hardware, trim pieces, and panel covers, expect prices to jump up to $100 per unit and even higher.

In an effort to save money on lights, check with friends who may be involved in commercial building demolition and/or remodeling. Many times, these construction professionals are faced with a myriad of building accessories that would cost more in man-hours to dismantle and sell than they are worth. In cases where professionals opt to tear out and discard dated but otherwise good light assemblies, you may be able to bargain with them and purchase those fixtures for a song.

Shop at local and even regional swap meets, flea markets, garage and estate sales, surplus liquidators, and stores going out of business. Look through classified ads under the heading of *Building Materials*. You might be surprised at how many listings offer fluorescent lights and other fixtures at very reasonable prices. At that, you might be able to get prices even lower by offering to purchase entire light inventories at one time.

While scouting around for a great deal on shop lights, keep your eyes open for bargains on packages of replacement bulbs and tubes. Home improvement centers frequently advertise boxes of 4ft and 8ft fluorescent tubes and various-watt incandescent bulbs at prices well below normal retail. Quantity lots purchased at below-retail prices will not only supply you with plenty of spares for later, but allow you to have some on hand for those used light fixtures that come without bulbs or tubes.

Accessory Lights

A variety of light fixtures is generally found in and around all automotive workshops. Complementing obvious overhead lights are units for storage closets, rest rooms, parts storage attics, office/research desk areas, outdoor porches, walkways, and carports.

For security, a lot of serious restorers and collectors install bright halogen outdoor motion detection lights on all four outside walls, as well as a few indoors. Motion detection lights should be wired into switches so they can be turned off during the day. Otherwise, they will constantly cycle on and off as they detect movement about your shop or around the yard.

One light style may not always serve every illumination purpose. Although fluorescent lights last the longest, use the least amount of electricity, and provide the most light, they don't necessarily work better than yellow incandescent bulbs for keeping bugs away from entry doors and porches at night. A row of incandescent lights mounted to a stylish light bar above a restroom sink may serve you better than an overhead fluorescent when trying to find a piece of dirt that has lodged in your eye.

The point behind mentioning such a variety of light fixtures and styles is not confusion, but rather to encourage you to shop around to get an overall idea of what is available to you. Measure different makes and models and take notes on which are most appealing. Then, with your graph paper and pencil, design a few different shop lighting layouts to see which will work best for your needs. Once you have narrowed your selection down to just a few options, you can begin shopping in earnest for the best bargains in town.

One of the best ways to dissuade potential thieves from casing or breaking into home-based workshops is to provide a great deal of nighttime illumination around such buildings. Flood lights used to be the best units for this purpose, but the increased brightness of outdoor halogen lights might prove them to be better options. If your shop is close to your house and you do not want constantly lit halogen lights shining into bedrooms at night, motion detection lights may be a good compromise. They are activated when they detect movement of people, dogs, deer, and other animals. Halogen lights are available in a number of different sizes designed to illuminate areas of specific dimensions.

CHAPTER 5

AIR PRESSURE SOURCES AND SETUP

Air compressors are almost a given for automotive workshops. Have you ever seen an auto repair facility without one? For years, auto restorers and repair professionals have regarded air compressors as mainstay shop equipment for the operation of pneumatic lifts, tire changers, heavy-impact wrenches, and similar units. Technological advances in tool and equipment designs have introduced hundreds of lightweight and high-speed pneumatically driven implements that can make auto restoration, repair, and maintenance much easier and quicker to accomplish.

In lieu of electrically operated power tools that are generally saddled with large, heavy motors and windings, auto repair professionals and enthusiasts are filling their shop cupboards, drawers, and tool chests with lighter and more convenient pneumatic power tools. Some of these include rotary and dual-action sanders, grinders, and metal cutters, ratchets, drills, flangers, and so on. Since power is supplied to these units through an independent air source, there is no need for them to include a heavy powerplant within their housings. This results in relatively lighter and slimmer tools.

Once you've decided to outfit your shop with an air compressor, spend time contemplating which tools and equipment it will most often be used to

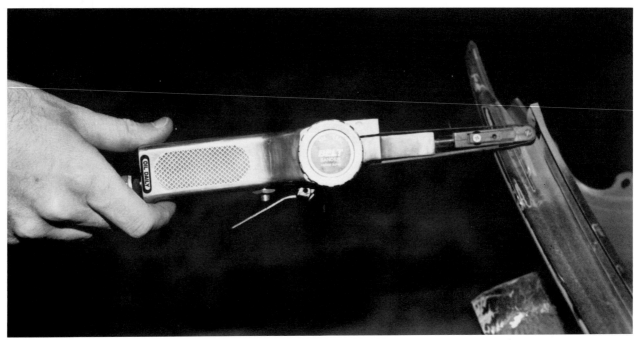

A pneumatically operated hand power tool is smaller and lighter than an equivalent electric model because it doesn't need a motor and windings inside its housing. Pneumatic tools' small size allows them to reach tighter working areas with plenty of power. An example is this pneumatic belt sander which can handily remove paint, rust, and scale from tight corners and along narrow grooves. Plan to outfit your automotive workshop with an air compressor and an assortment of air tools to help your repair and restoration projects progress efficiently.

power. Then, read labels or operating instructions for those units to determine how much air will be needed to operate them. In other words, do not go out and purchase just any air compressor that happens to be on sale. Realistically assess your air needs and then select a compressor that will supply the cubic feet per minute (cfm) and pounds per square inch (psi) required for your most demanding piece of equipment.

Cubic Feet Per Minute (cfm) Requirements

Compressed air must be supplied to tools and equipment at specific pressures and volume. Pressure is measured in pounds per square inch, and volume is rated at cubic feet per minute. Although a very small air compressor may be able to supply 80psi to tools, it may not have the capacity to provide the cfm needed to keep certain tools operating correctly. Once the trigger is pulled on a tool that needs 7cfm, the 80psi pressure on a small compressor might rapidly drop and stay low until that tool is turned off and the compressor has a chance to build its air supply back up to an original pressure level.

This aspect of an air compressor's pressure and volume relationship can be compared to that of a water spigot and hose. Open the spigot just a quarter turn, and only a little water comes out. Hold your thumb over the end of the hose, and pressure will certainly build up until a tiny, powerful stream squirts out. As long as you hold your thumb over the end of the hose, a very small amount of water comes out at high pressure. Once your thumb is moved to allow more volume, the pressure immediately drops, and just a dribble of water flows out. However, once the spigot is opened all the way, plenty of water at good pressure comes out with no problem.

Small air compressors can be likened to a water spigot opened only a quarter of a turn, and larger compressors more closely correspond to that spigot as it is opened further. A small, 1hp air compressor may be able to adequately supply one pneumatic tool for a short time before the tool must be turned off to allow the compressor's air tank to refill. A 3hp compressor is better, and is fine for most hobbyist activities and small repair projects. However, it will require the power and air tank storage capacity of a full 5hp air compressor to sustain any serious auto restoration or repair endeavor. To put this all in perspective, it may help to know that professional auto body repair shops consider 10hp air compressors absolute minimum standards.

To get a good idea of the cfm capacity your air compressor will need to generate in order to sufficiently supply the tools and equipment expected to outfit your shop, visit an auto body paint and supply store or read through an automotive tool and equipment catalog like The Eastwood Company's. Learn first-hand what the psi and cfm requirements are for the pneumatic tools and equipment you will be using. Expect to see ratings of 90psi and 4cfm for small

die grinders and ratchets, up to 80psi and 15cfm for some sandblasters.

Once you determine the cfm/psi needs for your shop, realize that you may want an air compressor that is capable of supplying more than that amount. If, for example, a 220V, 5hp air compressor can supply 10cfm at 90psi, and you have determined that your needs are right at 10cfm at 90psi, then this air compressor will have to operate constantly in order to keep up with the air supply demand. As the compressor continues to run, it will get hot enough to cause an abnormal amount of moisture to build up inside its storage tank. Moisture in air lines is bad news. Unless it is trapped in a dryer or water separator, moisture will spit out the ends of pneumatic tools or cause terrible problems with paint sprays.

Ideally, an air compressor should cycle off and on periodically, but never run continuously for much more than three or four minutes without equally spaced or longer intervals of rest between. An air compressor capable of supplying more air than required by the tools it is operating will only run for a few minutes and then shut down for a longer period. Rest times allow compressors to cool off, greatly reducing the amount of moisture introduced into related air system piping.

The air compressor at Dan Mycon's Newlook Autobody in Kirkland, Washington, has to supply the

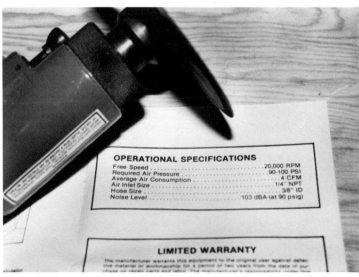

Air tool operating instructions include information regarding pounds per square inch (psi) and cubic feet per minute (cfm) requirements. This rotary sander, for example, operates best at 90–100psi with 4cfm. Supplied with less air pressure and volume than recommended, the tool cannot be expected to operate with maximum efficiency. Read instructions provided with air tools so that air regulators can be set to appropriate pressure levels each time tools are used. Store instructions in your tool chest drawers or other places where they are easily located should you ever need to verify settings.

needs of a number of auto body technicians and painters. At any given time, a couple of pneumatic sanders, buffers, grinders, and paint guns may be in operation simultaneously. This situation requires the power of a large 10hp-plus air compressor—an expensive machine.

On the other hand, a person who works out of a home garage or shop may only encounter a few occasions when more than one pneumatic tool is used at any one time. Realizing that many pneumatic hand tools only require 4cfm at 90psi, it stands to reason that a 5hp air compressor with a rating of 10cfm at 90psi could easily supply two such tools simultaneously. With that in mind, 5hp air compressors are probably the smallest units that will adequately serve the pneumatic needs of most small- to medium-sized workshops.

This large-capacity air compressor at Dan Mycon's Newlook Autobody is responsible for supplying working air pressure to a number of autobody technicians and painters who may be using a variety of air tools simultaneously. The unit was installed outdoors so it would not occupy valuable workshop space, and to reduce the noise pollution inside the shop. The structure built around this compressor is equipped with a key lock for security and screened sides for ventilation.

Air Compressor Tanks

Portable air compressors mounted on wheels and equipped with handles seldom have tanks with capacities larger than 30gal. These units generally supply plenty of air for most tools and some small pieces of equipment, but may become overtaxed when it comes to supplying much more than 5cfm at 90psi for prolonged periods. Although a 5hp compressor may be perfectly capable of supplying that amount of air, its 30gal supply tank is just too small to keep up with that demand.

Unless you need the mobility of a portable air compressor to serve other functions, consider stationary units with larger tanks. Instead of settling for a portable model's maximum tank capacity of 30gal, you could opt for either a vertical or horizontal stationary tank with 60gal or 80gal capacity. This would greatly enhance your air supply volumes and limit the need for your compressor to work more than necessary. Most experienced auto restorers regard 5hp compressors with 80gal tanks ideal units for general purposes because they have the ability to supply most sandblasters with appropriate air demands.

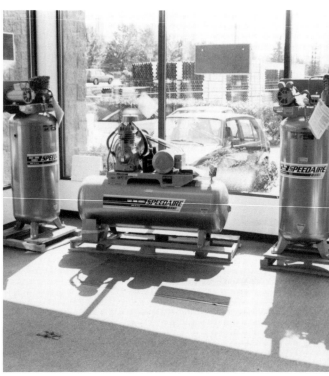

Air compressors and tanks are available in various sizes. Small, portable compressors mounted on wheels are generally limited to motors of about 5hp and 30gal tanks, while stationary models can range to 10hp and more, with tanks from 60–80gal or larger. Upright tanks require less floor area than horizontal models, whereas horizontal units may fit nicely inside ventilated closets built under stairways and other short spaces. A 5hp air compressor, coupled with an 80gal tank, should serve all of the needs of most active, home-based, automotive workshops.

Air Compressor Locations

John Roberts has been intrigued with automobiles ever since his childhood. For the past twenty-five years he has been a serious enthusiast and avid restorer of 1955–1957 Chevys. Most of his restoration activities have been conducted in a workshop behind his home in Bothell, Washington. Along with wanting to minimize shop noise for family members in the house, he also wanted to listen to his favorite music while working on cars. Early on during the outfitting of his shop, he realized that the old air compressor he had acquired and restored was going to be much too loud for him, his music, and his family.

This dilemma was resolved for everyone when Roberts built a separate little closet for the air compressor. Behind a solid core door and 6in walls filled with insulation, his 1929 heavy-duty air compressor can make as much noise as it wants without bothering anyone. Air is pumped through a series of pipes to outlets scattered about his shop for the convenient use of an assortment of air tools.

Permanent air compressor locations should be well thought-out. You must take their noisy operation into account, as well as their tendency to create moisture inside air lines. Accessibility for required preventive maintenance is also a concern. If your shop consists of a garage attached to your home, do not place a compressor next to a wall that separates the house and shop. Compressor noise could easily penetrate the house and disturb those family members who are trying to watch television, converse, or sleep. In this case, a place along an exterior wall would be better, and a small outbuilding attached to that exterior wall might be best.

Air compressors can certainly be located outdoors, as long as they are protected from the weather with a roof and walls. A small structure like a dog house should work fine for most installations. Security is a concern that could be put to rest with a locking door. Be sure the house you build for your compressor is equipped with screens or large doors that can be propped open to allow plenty of airflow through it and to the compressor.

One major consideration when contemplating an outdoor air compressor site is freezing weather and the accumulation of moisture inside air compressor motors and tanks. Moisture could freeze and plug air lines or cause damage to other internal mechanisms. For those living where winter temperatures frequently hover near or below freezing for extended periods of time, talk with a service representative from a commercial equipment dealer carrying a line of industrial air compressors. One can be found in the yellow pages under the heading of *Compressors—Air & Gas*.

Regardless of an air compressor location, you must accommodate its site with a compatible electrical outlet and enough electricity to power a unit. Small compressors,1hp up to some 3hp, will operate from a 110V, common household current. Compres-

John Roberts purchased this 1929 air compressor at an auction for a song. He rebuilt the unit years ago, and it has operated perfectly ever since with just routine maintenance. One problem he did discover early on, though, was that this compressor made a lot of noise every time it turned on. To solve that, he built an insulated closet around the compressor.

Air compressors located outdoors must be protected by some kind of structure. Because vandalism is not a problem around Bill Snyder's shop, a secure structure was unwarranted. A windward side wall and roof offer sufficient protection for his compressor. In regions where temperatures commonly drop below freezing for extended periods of time, outdoor air compressor structures should enclose units completely and be outfitted with insulation and a means to keep temperatures above freezing inside the housings. This might be accomplished by installing an incandescent light fixture or two inside the enclosures and keeping the bulbs lit throughout winter. Be certain that bulbs are not mounted too close to materials that could suffer heat damage.

sors with greater capacities require 220V supplies. With electricity and dedicated outlets as givens, consider the installation of an on/off switch as an excellent addition.

Air compressor units, fittings, lines, couplings, and the tools they serve are not always completely air tight—some leak. These leaks will cause an air compressor to turn on and off throughout the night to maintain its air pressure at the setting designated on its regulator. If your shop is located anywhere near your home or neighbors', chances are you or they will most definitely hear this compressor running in the dead of night. A handy on/off switch will eliminate that problem, as long as you remember to flip it off when you leave your shop.

Air Supply Systems

A small, portable air compressor might serve a great many needs for a one-person shop that consists mainly of a single-car garage. An auto hobbyist might be able to get by with a similar compressor in a larger shop, but avid restorers will need greater air supplies to support their arsenals of pneumatic tools and equipment. Instead of relying on sets of long air hoses stretched from your stationary compressor out to various work areas, plan to install an air piping system with outlets positioned at specific, high-use work stations.

Air systems have been installed successfully using galvanized, copper, or plastic pipe. Plumbing can be installed inside walls and then covered with dry-

Large, plastic-coated hooks, commonly available at hardware stores and home improvement centers, are perfect implements for the storage of coiled air hoses. Along with handy hose hooks, plan to outfit your workshop with plenty of actual air hose outlets. With numerous air connections available, you will not have to run great lengths of hose long distances from your compressor. Shorter lengths of air hose are much easier to manage.

Garry Allen has experienced no problems with the plastic pipe used for his air compressor supply system. He made sure that the pipe purchased was plenty strong enough to withstand the amount of air pressure to which it would be exposed, and put pipe sections and connections together exactly as recommended by the manufacturer, with lots of wall-mounted clamps to keep the system securely supported. Automotive paint manufacturers and others in the auto paint field recommend air supply pipe be no smaller than 3/4in in diameter. In lieu of plastic pipe, many auto professionals and avid enthusiasts have installed air systems using copper or galvanized pipe.

wall or mounted on finished wall surfaces. About the only concern would be leaks; it requires a lot more work to fix leaks in pipes buried behind walls. Pipe size is an important consideration. Small diameter pipe somewhat restricts air flow and can cause significant pressure loss between an air compressor and outlets positioned 20ft and farther away. Consider 3/4in inside-diameter pipe as the minimum. It is big enough to handle good air flows without causing noticeable pressure drops in reasonable runs from about 20–30ft. For large compressors that must serve numerous outlets simultaneously, plan to use 1in inside-diameter pipe.

A short section of flexible (rubber) hose should be used to make the connection between your compressor and the piping system. This hose will absorb and flow along with the vibrations made by your compressor as its motor operates, and not conduct that vibration into the pipe's support wall. Hard pipe connected directly to a compressor will carry vibrations into walls, eventually leading to loose pipe brackets, cracked drywall, and other problems.

As soon as your design will allow, run a main vertical feeder line straight up the wall to within 6in of the ceiling. Then, install successive horizontal pipes at a slight downward angle away from the compressor. This will allow any condensation in a horizontal line to drain toward an air dryer or trap located at the end of it. At each point along this main horizontal feeder where an outlet is planned at work-

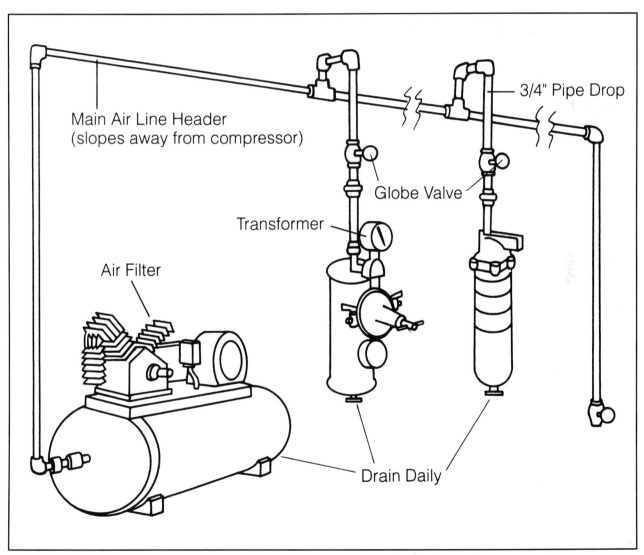

This illustration from PPG's Refinish Manual shows how air supply systems should be set up. Pipe 3/4in in diameter should rise from an air compressor, run to the ceiling, and then slope away from the compressor. Outlets are served from independent lines that come off the top of main hori- zontal feeders so that condensation and debris does not automatically flow down to them. The installation of any air transformers, dryers, water traps, or moisture separators will greatly help to ensure that the air delivered to your pneumatic tools and spray paint guns is dry and clean. PPG

bench level, install a "T" fitting. Position this "T" so that its center coupling faces up. Continue with the horizontal feeder until all outlet locations are outfitted with a "T," and at the very end install an elbow which faces down. This elbow should be equipped with a pipe that runs down to waist level and ends with a water trap or device used to drain water.

Back at the "T" fittings, attach a short piece of pipe that extends to about 3in above the horizontal feeder. To that, connect an elbow and then a 1in or 2in pipe that points away from the wall and out toward the shop area. At the end of this short pipe, install an elbow that faces down toward the planned outlet. Finish with a downward pipe to the outlet site, an elbow pointing out toward the shop, and then a female hose coupling.

Although it will require extra work to install a "T" and elbows at the top of main feeder lines, the effort will prove most worthwhile when you notice how dry the air is when it exits outlets. As warm, moist air flows from a compressor through feeder lines, it cools and turns into a liquid. If a pipe "T" simply pointed down from a horizontal feeder, this moisture would quickly flow right down to the outlet. A "T" that points up will prevent moisture from entering an outlet line and, therefore, moisture will be forced to continue running down the main horizontal feeder until it comes to the end of the line and a trap. Along with preventing moisture and condensation from entering outlets directly, this system will also help direct oil and other debris down main feeders to specific drains or traps.

Air Outlets

Could any automotive workshop ever have too many air outlets? Well, that depends on the type of work planned for the shop and the number of pneumatic tools employed. Auto body and paint shops require plenty of air pressure for sanders, grinders, buffers, and spray paint guns. An engine rebuilder may need less pressure to supply air ratchets, die grinders, and blow gun tips. However, should you install a minimal number of air outlets initially, you can

John Roberts' friends teased him about buying an old pneumatic tire changer from an auction held at a gasoline service station. They figured he would never use it. He smiled politely then, and has for years—every time those same friends have brought over wheels that needed tire changes. Since you will never know what type of pneumatic tool or equipment you might bring back to your shop someday, it would be in your best interest to provide your workshop with many compressed air outlets that could conveniently serve such items as old tire changers.

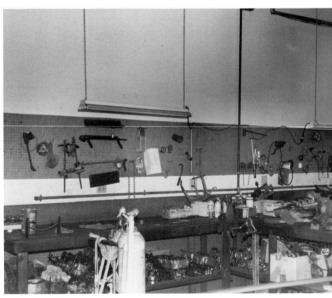

This long workbench at Jack Holden's Champion Import Service is outfitted with a number of compressed air outlets. Notice that the main air supply comes from ceiling level. Although you may only be able to use one air tool at a time, even when more than one are needed, it is quite inconvenient to have to uncouple one and hook up the other every time different tools are used. Therefore, plan to outfit your workbenches with two, three, or four air outlets so tools can remain hooked up during entire repair operations. You may even consider storing several short air hose sections next to these outlets for added convenience.

bet that sooner or later you will want just one more somewhere to accommodate a new tool, workbench, or shop addition.

Air outlets located at both ends of a workbench are very handy. They can each supply tools being used near them, of course, but together they allow you the opportunity to have two tools hooked up and ready to work simultaneously. If, for example, you were cleaning up an engine block and needed both a die grinder with burrs to file away casting slag and a blow gun to clean out debris, you could have both units hooked up at the same time. This negates a need to disconnect the die grinder and connect the blow gun and then reverse the process afterward. Sounds simple, but it sure is handy.

An outlet located on a center post between two bay doors will serve tire filling needs for vehicles parked in stalls as well as those parked outdoors. Ceiling-mounted air hose reels or coils are ideal for work under hoods and on roofs. Will one bay in your shop be designated as a paint booth? Plan to have an outlet at the front of it to accommodate spray paint guns. A tire changer will require air, and you should have an outlet near it. If you plan to construct a carport alongside your shop for vehicle storage, why not locate an outlet there? Vehicles stored for any length of time frequently suffer tire pressure loss, and an air hose at that location might serve you well when it comes time to remove leaves, dust, and debris that have settled on vehicles over time.

Air outlets are similar to electrical outlets. They are needed to power tools and equipment that are, in turn, required for the completion of specific automotive work. You could certainly get by with just one outlet and a very long air hose or electrical extension cord, but who wants to? In lieu of long extension cords, install plenty of electrical outlets. Same for air. Instead of relying upon one or two long hoses that can easily stretch from one end of your shop to the other—while getting all tangled up and snarled in between—why not opt for a number of outlets close to work areas, each equipped with its own hose?

Air Regulators and Dryers

Air compressors are commonly outfitted with their own pressure regulators. These devices adjust air pressure at the compressor's outlet to whatever setting is designated. Should your compressor normally fill its tank to 100psi, you can regulate the pressure at the tank's outlet to any level desired, from 1psi clear through to 100psi. This is fine for operations undertaken within very short distances of the compressor. However, especially for spray painting, air pressure at tool tips must be set very close to manufacturers' recommendations.

Remember that smaller inside-diameter pipes can cause reductions in air pressure? Well, the greater the distance that air must travel through pipes, the more susceptible it is to pressure loss—virtually regardless of pipe size. To compensate, painters and other professional auto technicians install individual air pressure regulators at those air outlets most frequently used. This way, they can set compressor regulators to pump out pressure over and beyond what is needed at tool tips, and then fine-tune actual working air pressure needs at the outlet which directly serves their paint guns or other pneumatic devices.

Air dryers and all of the implements designed to remove moisture from air lines are critically important for every painting job. Water and paint do not mix. Any moisture contamination in air lines that serve paint sprayers will cause paint to bubble, run, and generally misbehave in manners totally inconsistent with professional paint finish expectations. Air that supplies paint guns must be dry and free from all contaminants.

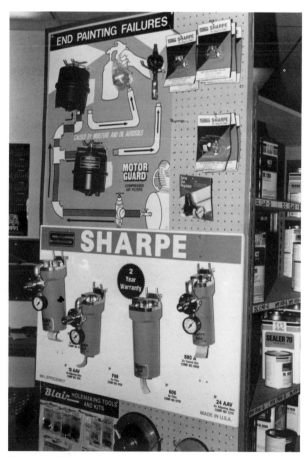

Compressed air supply systems, properly set up with sloping feeders and outlet lines that come off of the tops of main feeders, are still susceptible to condensation and contamination. Therefore, plan to install a series of air filters and dryers in these lines to ensure moisture does not infiltrate spray paint guns and other pneumatic tools. You should be able to locate a wide variety of filters, dryers, and regulators at autobody paint and supply stores and retail outlets which carry air compressors and pneumatic equipment.

81

Moisture, oil, and other debris in air lines will also hinder the operation of other pneumatic tools. Water spitting out of a sander won't do much to help the restoration procedure; oil contamination could surely botch paint buffing operations; and grinders normally do their best work without liquid debris pouring out of their exhaust ports. Every pneumatic tool is designed for use that consists of dry air supplies delivered at designated psi and cfm. Dryers, water separators, and traps are designed to provide specific protection against such contaminants.

If your air piping system has been set up correctly with regard to sloping feeder pipes and upright outlet line diversions, you should only need air dryers at those outlets which serve painting equipment. Grinders, sanders, ratchets, and other pneumatic tools will operate fine with some minute traces of moisture in their supply lines, but paint guns will not. If ever in doubt, simply attach an air dryer or water separator to your air outlet to ensure a pneumatic tool's best operation.

Overview

The advent of so many pneumatic tools has made the jobs of auto restoration, repair, and maintenance much easier for just about everyone. Not only are these tools much lighter and easier to handle, they operate at efficient speeds and accomplish a great deal of work in little time. It may take some users more time than others to adjust to their maneuvers, but overall they are great time- and work-savers.

While building and outfitting an automotive workshop, make sure you talk to lots of avid and active auto enthusiasts to find out what they have learned about air-powered equipment. Maybe their shop's air compressor, rated at 8hp, is still too small to accommodate all of their needs, and they would relish replacing it with a 10hp model. Their shop's air outlet locations might be too few and they would now prefer to have additional ones in places you never considered.

Long, straight air hoses work great for most applications, but would coiled hoses function better next to workbenches and ceiling mounts? What kinds of obstacles do you expect in your shop? Will it be filled with three or four cars most of the time? Or will it be strictly used for one-car restoration projects? These are questions you must ask yourself in order to design an air system that will function most effectively for you.

All in all, an air compressor with a few hoses and key tools will save you time and trouble. An air compressor is a good investment, and by planning ahead to maximize its capabilities, you will do nothing but improve your shop's working environment.

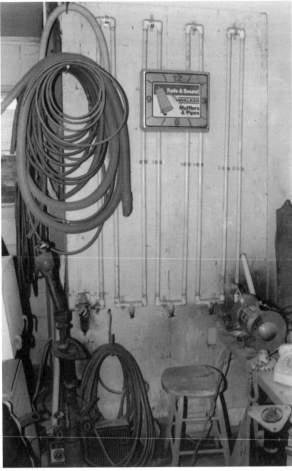

John Roberts installed this series of radiator-like piping lines to trap and drain moisture from his compressed air supply system. As air is forced through these pipes, it cools and moisture in that air condenses into liquid. The liquid is drained off through petcocks installed at the base of each vertical pipe run. To further ensure dry air for his paint guns and air tools, Roberts also installed an air filter/moisture separator at the end of this line to trap any contaminants that may have gotten by his pipe trap system. Roberts reports that he has never experienced any moisture or contamination problems with this compressed air supply system.

CHAPTER 6

WORKBENCHES

An automotive workshop could be big enough to accommodate numerous vehicles and lots of equipment, have plenty of light and a super compressed-air supply system, but would lack a great deal of convenience if it were not outfitted with workbenches. Without a workbench or table, where would repair and maintenance take place for parts like carburetors, alternators, heads, distributors, and so on?

One small, 6ft long workbench may serve the needs of an auto hobbyist limited to working out of a single-car garage, but avid enthusiasts need more. An ideal auto workshop design might feature three, four, and more workbench areas along walls. Narrow workbenches or tables about 12in to 18in wide, lo-

Small workbenches, with storage beneath and a place to hang tools, may be fine for auto hobbyists who have no desires beyond regular maintenance work. Conversely, those with active interests in automotive repair and restoration will require substantially larger workbenches to accommodate the wide variety of tasks. This workbench design can be expanded from this basic, 4ft long model, to units as long as desired. It is important for you to envision the types of activities likely to be undertaken in your workshop so that appropriate workbenches may be planned and installed.

Tool chests, storage cabinets, and workbenches are primary automotive workshop accessories. Without them, one would have a difficult time accomplishing much in the way of auto repair and restoration. Workbenches do not have to be custom-designed or expensive. Quite simply, they are places where repair work can be performed on small- to medium-sized items and where parts, tools, and supplies may be set until one has the opportunity to put them away.

cated between parking stalls and outfitted with open shelves under bench tops, could prove quite useful for repair efforts along vehicle sides—assuming that plenty of room still remains for opening car doors and working around them. Almost any workbench setup will enhance shop convenience, as long as units do not interfere with space for vehicle maneuvering or hinder other repair work.

How many times have you tried to set a part down on a little workbench only to find it covered with an array of tools, car parts, rags, empty parts packages, cans of screws and bolts, extension cords, and everything else under the sun? You could always take time to put everything away as soon as you are done with it, but what if numerous implements are required for repair operations underway? To help eliminate headaches associated with cluttered workbench tops, plan to complement workbenches with storage shelves and/or drawers under their work surfaces for large items, and then install cupboards or shelves above for hand tools, miscellaneous cans, shop towels, and what have you.

Workbenches do not have to be fancy, but they must be strong. Many of the auto parts you will repair on workbenches will be heavy, and you will probably find occasions where some pounding may be needed. So, plan to build workbenches out of sturdy 2x4, 2x6, and larger lumber, along with plywood that is at least 3/4in thick. Metal workbenches are fine, too. But be sure they are constructed with strong sections of angle iron and plate steel.

Does this look familiar to you? How many times have you wanted to set down a few packages of new auto parts or tools only to find your meager workbench overflowing with stuff? Consider building shelves or cabinets above workbenches to store frequently used items or supplies so that actual workbench surfaces can remain free for repair work. Simple shelves are made from 12in wide strips of 3/4in plywood placed on top of prefabricated brackets commonly sold at hardware stores, lumber yards, and home improvement centers. For wood frame walls, use 3in or longer cabinet screws to secure brackets. On concrete block walls you will need to drill holes with a masonry bit, insert appropriate anchors, and then screw in compatible lag screws or bolts.

Workbench placement requires forethought. Simply sticking long workbenches here and there will ultimately result in a cluttered workshop. Realize that a great deal of the room in your shop will be taken up by vehicles parked in it. Then, logically envision where there is the greatest need for workbenches. This should result in the accommodation of both workbench convenience and space requirements around project vehicles. This is a handy workbench set up in an alcove area behind the restroom in Garry Allen's shop. This space stays relatively dust-free, and is perfect for engine head work and other tasks.

Placement

A workshop's overall floor plan will generally offer certain sites ideal for workbench placement. Alcoves along exterior walls, set in and away from the edge of parking stalls, are generally perfect for wall-length workbenches. If an alcove is deep enough, a 3ft-wide workbench surface may be a viable option. Although considered quite big, this size could be very useful when working on bare engine blocks and other large items.

Spaces at the front of parked vehicles are always handy for workbenches. Placed there, workbenches are perfect for engine tune-ups and other underhood chores. Serving as convenient storage shelves for air cleaners and new parts replacements, they also keep engine diagnostic equipment, wrenches, ratchets, and sockets close at hand. These sites could also prove useful when it comes time to yank out old generators or other accessories and complete their repair or restoration.

Mike Holiman's shop is designed with two parking stalls and a separate section off to the side that is equal in floor area to a single-car garage. This area is outfitted with a wall-length workbench, storage shelves, and a large work table positioned as an island between this space and a parking stall. The table's placement is such that Holiman can use either side at any time. Because it is virtually out in the open, this table is great for working on motors, transmissions, and other large assemblies.

A small work place next to a telephone might be useful. Here, you could store not only telephone books, but also parts catalogs and other reference materials needed when ordering parts and supplies. A counter or desk near a telephone could double as a research center for reading manuals in efforts to restore classics to original condition and Concours d'Elegance perfection.

Workbenches should be constructed with features that best serve the work planned for specific ar-

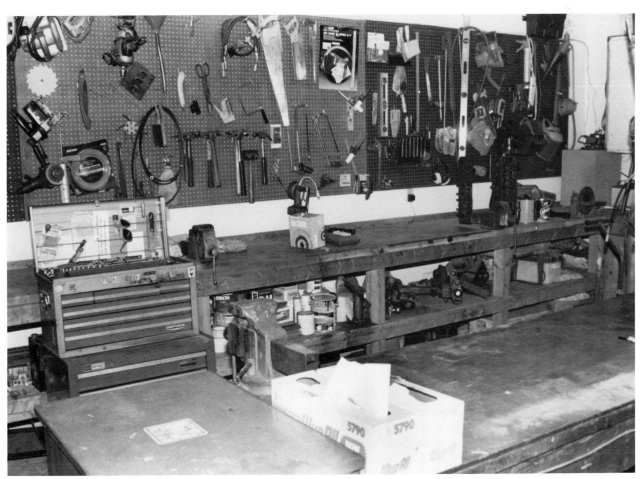

Holiman set up about one-third of his auto workshop with workbenches, storage, and a work table. He has found the work table a fine shop feature, especially when reassembling engines and transmissions. A simple walk around this table offers him a 360 degree view of the project at hand without having to move anything. His tool chest on wheels is filled with frequently used hand tools and is rolled around the shop to the sites of large repair or maintenance projects.

Workbenches constructed with sturdy lumber should be expected to hold up to a wide variety of work. Likewise, users can outfit these workbenches with specific features to expand their overall capabilities. Holiman installed a thick sheet of steel plate on top of this workbench and uses it as a makeshift welding, general metalworking, and hammer pounding site.

Almost every workbench should be outfitted with a bottom shelf. These spaces serve as convenient storage spots for small welders, plasma cutters, tool boxes, and a host of other things. If your shop is cluttered with several pieces of portable equipment consider eliminating such shelves in lieu of storage areas for those items. At the least, make use of the space beneath workbenches for something more than just dust accumulation.

eas. Next to a welding booth, for example, a workbench with a metal surface could handle hot items freshly welded, and a small anvil mounted nearby may be perfect for hot metalworking tasks. This workbench should be outfitted with storage units for most of the tools, equipment, and supplies regularly used during metalworking operations.

If your interests mainly focus around auto body and paint work, design a workbench and storage system in the area where most of those activities will take place. This would likely be a space where welders, grinders, sanders, and other auto body repair implements are stored. If one stall in your shop is used as a primary paint booth, plan to locate a small workbench close by so that it can store masking and painting supplies and also be used for mixing paint. Design cupboards or drawers with hooks, so that spray paint guns can be stored upright and behind doors to prevent shop dust from infiltrating their ports and passageways.

A workshop's dimensions may prohibit the installation of workbenches in certain areas. One such situation entails a narrow shop where the distance from a bay door to the far parallel wall may be less than 20ft. Most large American pickup trucks and cars measure close to 18ft long. A workbench at the front of a stall would force a parked pickup truck's bed to stick out of the bay door. Shallow shops, therefore, should be outfitted with workbenches along their side walls thus leaving space at the fronts of vehicles for working and maneuvering.

Use graph paper and a ruler to draw out a workbench placement plan. Use a 1/4in per foot scale to pencil in workbench dimensions that are compatible with vehicles expected to be parked in stalls and with large equipment mounted separately to the floor. Every 1/4in increment on paper will equal a full foot in your shop; 1in on paper will equal 4ft of actual distance. Actually measure cars, equipment, and other large shop accessories, and pencil them in at the 1/4in scale. Be sure to maintain aisles at least 3ft wide, and account for spaces that car doors will occupy when opened.

Size

Plywood is manufactured in sheets 4ft wide and 8ft long. Construction lumber, like 2x4s and 2x6s, is sold at even lengths: 4ft, 6ft, 8ft, and so on. Therefore, workbenches built to even length and width dimensions normally result in the least amount of wood material waste. A similar situation exists with metal, although scrap metal yards may offer an abundance of angle iron and plate steel in a variety of sizes.

Length

General use workbenches should be built to the maximum lengths allowed by shop designs and the location of large equipment units. A working surface 8ft long will accommodate much more activity than one 6ft in length. Long workbenches provide plenty of space for laying out disassembled parts and working with odd shaped items like trim, axles, drive lines, linkage arms, and the like.

A large work surface will enable you to have a number of hand and power tools out in the open for easy access while you are involved with specific repair operations. For the most part, big workbenches are very useful for a wide assortment of activities, whereas short models limit repair projects to only those auto parts that can fit on them.

Your shop's actual free wall space will greatly impact workbench lengths. Try to fit in at least one 8ft or longer workbench that will accommodate big repair jobs and double as a large surface where parts can be entirely disassembled and laid out in specific sections or sequences.

Height

Workbench height is an important consideration. Most desks are around 30in high, and kitchen counters stand at about 36in. People 6ft tall and taller may prefer workbench surfaces that are 40in or more off the ground so that they do not have to constantly stoop while working. Conversely, shorter people

might want to build their workbenches to heights better matching their needs.

You can easily determine a perfect working height for your workbenches simply by measuring different counters and tables around your home and shop. Do you have a tool chest which features a flat work area? How do you like working at its height? Are your kitchen counters set at a comfortable level? Would an inch or two higher or lower make much of a difference? If they are too high, stand on a telephone book or an encyclopedia and see if the added height would increase your comfort. If they are too short, stack up some thick books and then lay a breadboard on top of them to judge how comfortable it would be for you to work at that level. Once you have arranged a makeshift work surface, measure the distance and plan to build your workbenches to that dimension.

Utility workbenches must accommodate the tools and equipment used on their surfaces. Here, a bench top drill press fits nicely on a narrow, wall-length workbench. Storage underneath could be enhanced with a shelf to keep items off of the floor. This space in Ron and Rick Weglin's shop is normally crowded with automobiles, limiting the width of any workbench located here. To offset that restriction, they opted for a long, narrow workbench.

If your work will entail a lot of intricate electric and soldering tasks, you may want to design a smaller and shorter workbench, about 30in high, that you can pull a chair up to and sit at. Likewise, a counter-like work surface raised higher might be perfect for use with a stool. Again, you have to project what types of jobs you will most likely undertake and then build work centers that can most efficiently and comfortably suit those needs for both standing and sitting positions.

Width

As with length and height, workbench width is determined by shop designs and user preference. Many kitchen counters measure 26in wide; older oak school teacher desks frequently feature 32in widths; and large picnic tables may be as wide as 36in. Once again, you are encouraged to measure some of the tables and counters around your home to see which widths are most accommodating for your size, your arm's reach, and expected work surface area requirements.

Workbench tops should seldom, if ever, be any less than 24in wide. A 30in width is more suitable, as it offers lots of working area without being too big for most people to work from. In close quarters, a narrow counter could be installed not so much for use as a work place but rather for the convenience of having a spot where new parts could be set down or books laid out for review. Such an installation might be made on top of a storage cabinet that rests about 2ft below cupboards installed above.

Designs

For the most part, workbenches are little more than heavy-duty tables. There is no universal workbench design. Many folks simply nail a 2x4 to the wall, attach short 2x4s to the ends of it so they stick out, nail 4x4 legs to those ends, and then nail another long 2x4 to the tops of those legs and cover it all with

This workbench was built with 2x4s and 3/4in plywood. The inside leg of the double upright 2x4s is a solid 3ft board. The front leg consists of a short upright support at the bottom with a cross brace above it, then a longer upright support with another cross brace above it. This is a simple, sturdy design that is very easy to construct. Along with offering a solid workbench surface, it has a full-length bottom shelf strong enough to support a welder, plasma cutter, and an host of other things.

This basic, heavy-duty workbench has been outfitted with extra storage shelves on the left and a 48x32in work top on the right. Storage underneath accommodates a wire feed welder, plasma cutter, large tool box, indoor vehicle exhaust system, and another large tool box—with plenty of room to spare. Pegboard and Sta-Put Hooks are ideal for hand tools. The entire unit measures 8ft long and 6-1/2ft tall, with a 28in wide lower shelf, 32in wide workbench top, and 20in wide upper shelves.

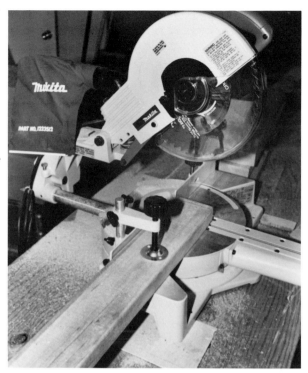

This Makita 10in Slide Compound Saw works fast and accurately to cut lumber up to 12in wide at any angle. It was used to precisely cut sections out of 2x4s to build the economical, heavy-duty workbench featured in the previous two photos. As important as it is to equip workshops with dependable automotive tools and equipment, it is equally important to utilize quality woodworking tools and equipment when constructing and outfitting these shops. As workshop owners use their shops for more and more projects, they often need to build more workbenches, cabinets, and other additions. Maintain an arsenal of reliable woodworking tools and equipment with sharp blades and bits to facilitate shop improvements.

After using a tape measure to locate the center of a 94-1/2in lower workbench long brace (47-1/4in), Jim Yocum marks a straight line with a square where that workbench center leg's left edge should be placed. Since 2x4 lumber actually measures 1-1/2in thick by 3-1/2in wide, he marked long, straight lines 1-3/4in away from the exact center of the 2x4 brace—thus ensuring the accurate placement of the 3ft long and 3-1/2in wide workbench center leg's left edge.

94 1/2" long brace		22" leg support
94 1/2" long brace		22" leg support
94 1/2" long brace		7" leg support / 7" leg support
94 1/2" long brace		7" leg support / 7" leg support
3' Leg	3' Leg	3' Leg / 7" leg support
3' Leg	3' Leg	3' Leg / 7" leg support
25' cross brace	25' cross brace	25' cross brace / 22" leg support / 22" leg support
25' cross brace	25' cross brace	25' cross brace / 22" leg support / 22" leg support

NOTE:
Dotted area
is waste

The basic frame for a sturdy 8ft long workbench can be constructed from eight 10ft long 2x4s. To minimize waste, cut 10ft 2x4s in the sequence illustrated above.

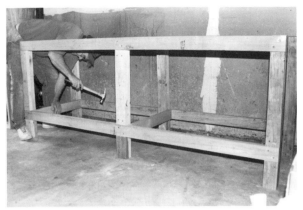

Once the workbench front and rear frames are built, use 16d nails to secure the lower 25in cross braces. Be careful when using feet and legs to brace boards being nailed, not only for wild and misplaced hammer swings, but also for long nails that may penetrate boards. Notice that these cross braces are positioned in line with the lower front and rear 2x4 braces.

A Makita table saw is used to cut a 4x8ft sheet of ACX plywood lengthwise into two separate 8ft long sheets: one measuring 28in wide; and the other 20in wide. The fence on this saw was set at 28in so that the largest portion of the plywood sheet was located between the blade and fence for stability. Since table saw blades cut from the top down, the best plywood side should be on top, so it suffers the least amount of edge splintering. Cutting full sheets of plywood on a table saw is awkward and requires at least two people. It may be best to use roller stands designed to support long materials being cut on a table saw. In lieu of a table saw, you can place plywood on top of four evenly spaced 2x4s and employ a cutting guide and a power circular saw. The 2x4s will support the plywood sheet in a flat and secure position during and after the cuts. Be sure the saw's base is adjusted such that the blade does not cut deeper than the plywood.

a sheet of plywood. This simple design may be fine for very lightweight tasks, but will never hold up to the rigors of active automotive repair and restoration.

A basic, heavy-duty, 3ft high by 8ft long by 32in wide workbench, with a shelf underneath and shelves above, can be made with eight 10ft long 2x4s, three 4x8ft sheets of 3/4in plywood, and one 4x8ft sheet of 3/8in plywood or 1/4in pegboard. Legs are made by doubling 2x4s (nailed together); 2x4s are also used as cross-brace supports. The workbench's top, sides, and both top and bottom shelves are made from 3/4in plywood. A sheet of 3/8in plywood or 1/4in thick pegboard covers the back. You will also need about four pounds of 16d nails and two pounds of 8d nails.

Basically, four 10ft 2x4s are cut to 94-1/2in; two are cut into six 36in pieces; and two are cut into six 25in pieces. The leftover material from all of the 2x4s is then used for additional members. The four 2ft pieces left over from the four cut at 94-1/2in are then cut to 22in, and two 22in boards are also cut from the two 3ft sections left over from cutting six 25in boards. From the remaining wood cut out six 7in boards. After all cuts are made you should end up with:

—four boards at 94-1/2in;
—six boards at 36in;
—six boards at 25in;
—six boards at 22in; and
—six boards at 7in.

The accompanying photos and captions detail the construction of this workbench.

The 28in wide sheet of plywood just cut will be used as a lower shelf for this workbench design. The remaining 20in section will be used for the workbench's top shelf. In order to fit between the workbench end panels, the 28in wide shelf must be trimmed to 94-1/2in, the same length as the 2x4 front and rear braces. A Makita 7-1/4in Hypoid Saw with a guide has been adjusted to trim the edge. Always properly position your hands when using power saws: one hand on the trigger handle and the other on the saw's upper handle.

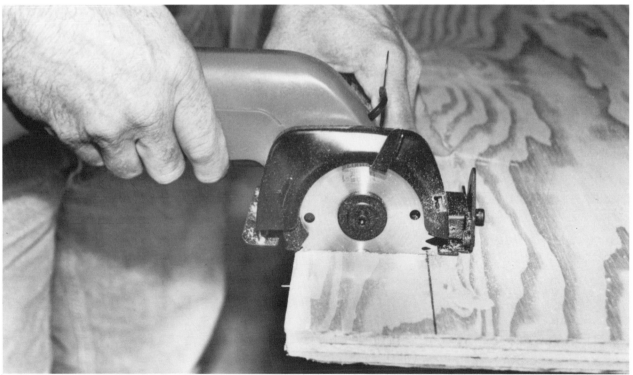

The bottom shelf of this workbench design must be notched at each corner and in the center in order to accommodate the six legs. Since this shelf will extend to the outer faces of the 2x4 side braces, it has been cut to 28in wide; this also includes a 3in width created by the workbench legs' double 2x4s (each 2x4 is 1-1/2in thick). Therefore, notches in the bottom shelf must each be 3-1/2in wide and 3in deep, cut precisely where the shelf's edge will make contact with the legs. You could lay the plywood shelf on top of the frame and mark notches, or rely on measurements to accurately mark notching lines. A small circular saw like this 3-1/8in Makita can be easier to use on small cuts like this.

Another sheet of 3/4in ACX plywood was cut into two sections, one measuring 32in wide and the other 16in wide. The 32in wide piece will serve as the workbench's top work surface, and the 16in wide piece will be used for upper shelves. Leave both pieces at their 8ft length for the time being; the 32in work surface piece will later be accurately notched to accommodate two vertical plywood side panels. The 16in wide shelving piece will be cut to whatever length may be desired for your workbench shelving needs.

The rearward side portion of the workbench top surface (32in wide plywood piece) has been notched to allow the rear portion of a vertical plywood side panel to fit flush against it. The front part of the vertical side panel will fit under the front, un-notched portion of the work surface for added support. The portion of the vertical side panel that fits flush with the notch will extend up and past the work surface to form a side for upper storage shelves.

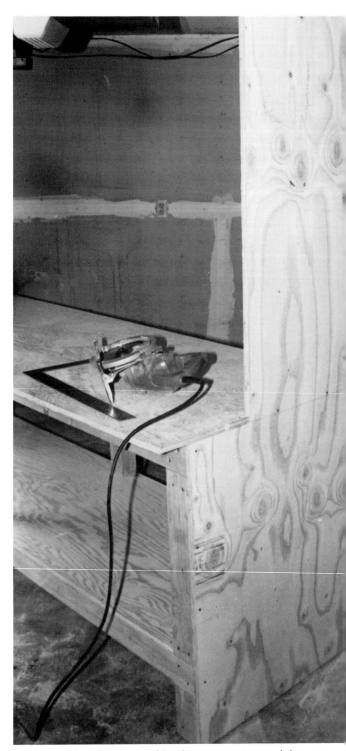

With a workbench side panel in place, you get a much better idea of what the overall assembly should look like. Notice that the notch made at the back of the workbench's top surface allows this side panel to extend up past the work surface to make for an ideal storage shelf assembly. The front portion of the side panel fits under the work surface for added support. Pencil marks made on this side panel and in line with the 3/4in plywood workbench top serve as a guide for where 8d nails are to be driven into the workbench top for added stability.

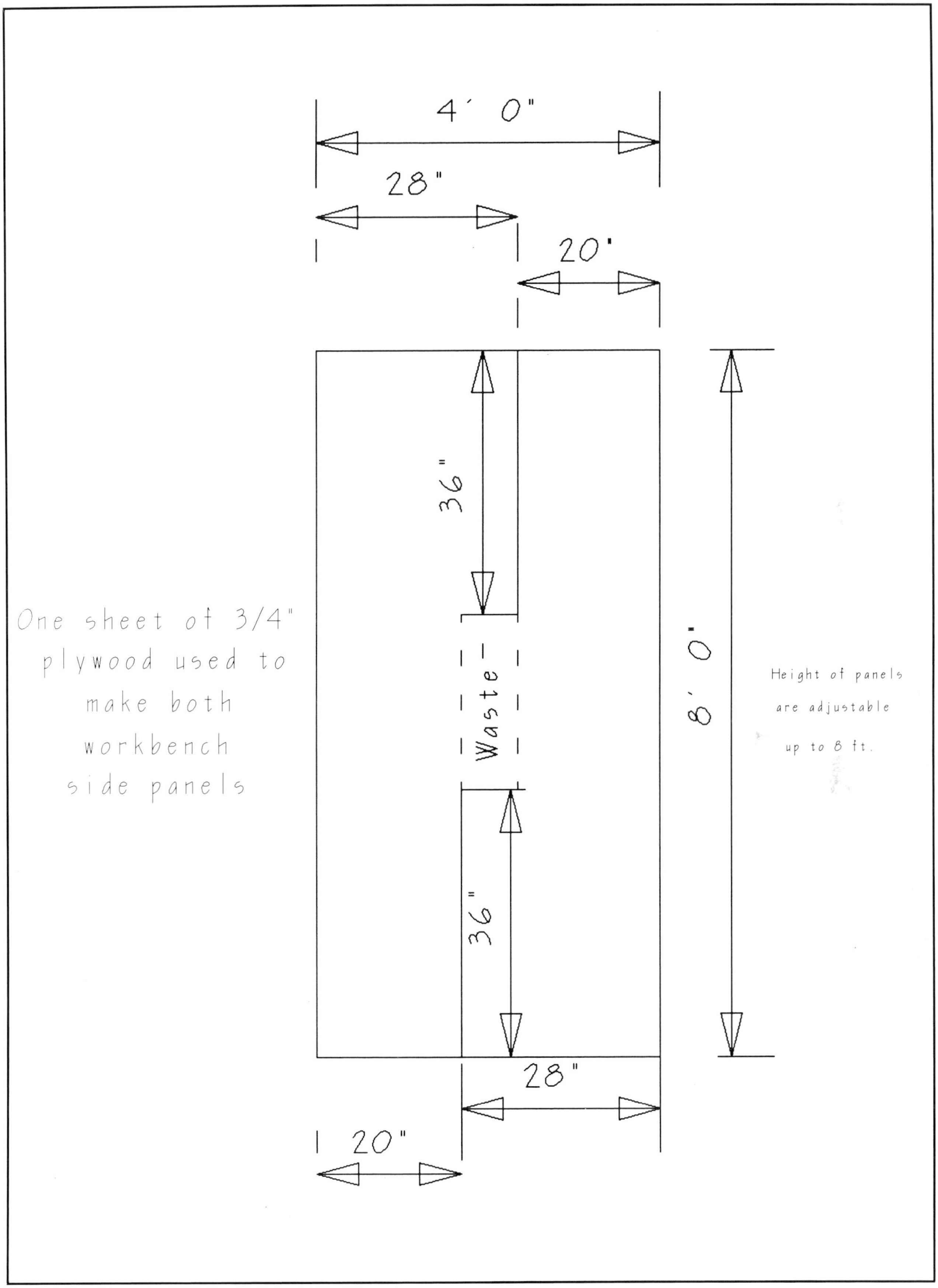

4' 0"

28"

20'

36"

One sheet of 3/4"
plywood used to
make both
workbench
side panels

Waste

36"

8' 0"

Height of panels
are adjustable
up to 8 ft.

28"

20"

93

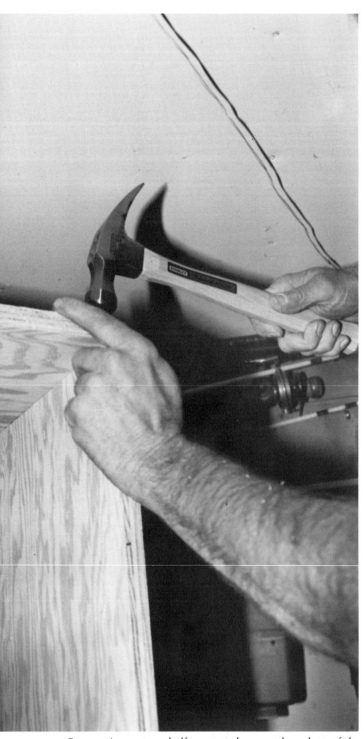

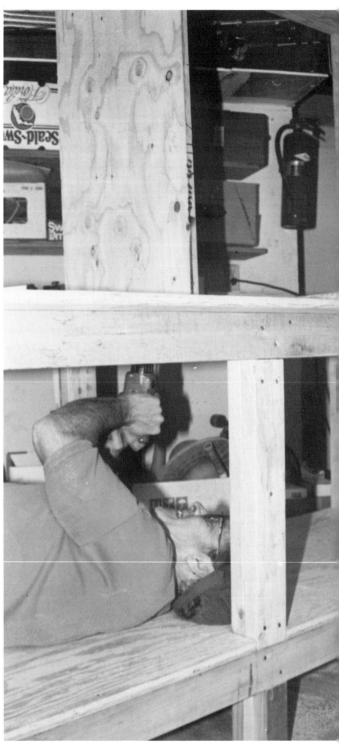

For maximum top shelf support, be sure the edges of the top shelf rest on top of and are nailed to the tops of the side panels. Vertical support(s) rising from the top of the work surface will supply needed support in the middle of the top shelf. Galvanized 8d or 6d finishing nails are used to secure the top shelf to the side panels. Finishing nails feature a small head that can be slightly driven into the plywood to create a small depression. The depressions are later filled with wood putty, allowed to dry, and then sanded smooth. The end result is the appearance that no nails were used to assemble the bench.

With both workbench side panels secured in place and the top 20in shelf nailed to them, Yocum uses a Makita drill/driver to drive a 2in wood screw through the work surface and into a vertical piece of plywood that will serve as a support for the middle of the top shelf. Measurements were taken and lines drawn to indicate where the three wood screws should be driven in order to hit the center of this middle support panel. This panel will not only help to support the top shelf, it will also serve as a side panel for additional shelves installed on one side of the workbench.

To facilitate the installation of cabinet and cupboard doors on workbenches and other storage units, plywood shelves, tops, bottoms, and panels must be outfitted with 1in wide, solid wood face-trim. This can be clearly visualized by looking at household kitchen and bathroom cabinets. A miter saw works great for cutting pine and other solid wood trim at precisely 90 degrees; be sure to use saw accessory hold-down mechanisms to ensure perfect cuts. Once a long piece of trim has been cut and secured along the top shelf, upright trim pieces are cut and secured with 6d finishing nails used on the top trim section. Use a nail set to force nail heads below face surfaces and fill in the voids with wood putty to make nails invisible after wood is stained or painted. A thin section of trim is used for the bottom shelf face so that it does not protrude into the open area underneath.

Workbench storage doors can be quickly designed so their back sides fit flush with face trim, or notched so that a portion of their back sides actually fits inside door openings. Plywood doors made from 3/4in plywood are plenty thick enough to accept both a rabbet (notched) edge and a rounded-off router edge. This extra custom work on doors will help to keep dust and contaminants out of cabinet areas and lend an appealing appearance to workbenches and cabinets outfitted with similar designs.

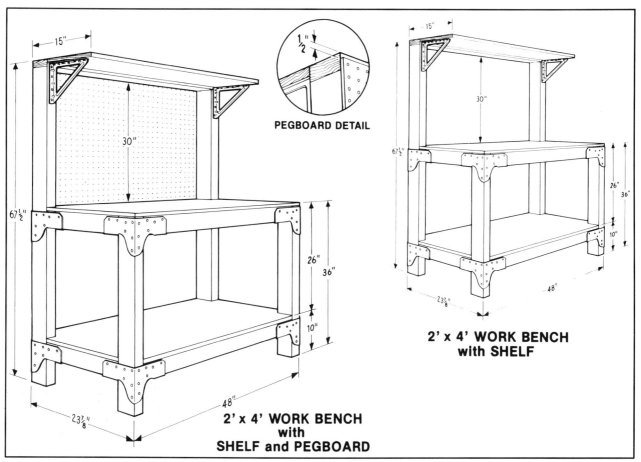

PEGBOARD DETAIL

2' x 4' WORK BENCH
with SHELF

2' x 4' WORK BENCH
with
SHELF and PEGBOARD

An alternative to the home-built workbench previously described is a unit like this that uses a combination of lumber and prefabricated corner pieces. Simpson Strong-Tie Company, Inc.

Weight Support Concerns

The workbench detailed on these pages should be plenty strong and sturdy for most automotive repair work. However, should you want something that is guaranteed to hold up under engine blocks, beefy automatic transmissions, and other heavy stuff, you might consider building a sturdier workbench—one with 4x4 legs on 3ft centers, 2x6 braces on each side of all legs, and a work surface made with 2x6s. A 3/4in plywood bottom shelf will help to hold it all together, too.

Work tables made out of angle iron and steel plate may be better suited for heavy engine and transmission work. In addition to its strength, metal is easier to clean, and will not absorb oil and transmission fluid like wood. Metal workbenches and tables can either be welded together or secured with large bolts, nuts, and lock washers.

Angle iron supports should run along the entire perimeter of steel-plate work surfaces. Plan to span angle iron or heavy square tubing supports beneath the workbench top at about 2ft on-center. Then attach heavy angle iron or square tubing legs no more than 3ft apart. Be sure to run support braces between

Metal workbenches offer a great deal of weight support when they are carefully assembled with heavy-duty bolts and screws. This one at Mathewson's Automotive & Tire has supported a lot of engines and transmissions without showing many signs of wear. Notice that this workbench is outfitted with a compressed air connection, a four-receptacle electric outlet, heavy-duty vise, and bench grinder, and allows room for plenty of storage underneath.

the legs to keep them secure. These braces should also make a nice frame for a lower shelf.

Surface Options

Bare plywood or lumber workbench tops will absorb oil, grease, and most other liquids. They will stain and become unsightly in short order unless primered and then painted, or treated to a quality clear sealer and left a natural color. If these options are not acceptable, you will have to outfit your workbench tops with a material that cleans easily, holds up under heavy weights, and will not chip or crack when heavy things are dropped on it.

Formica looks good on counters, cleans easily, and holds up well under lightweight use, but it would probably crack or chip under normal automotive repair operations. A thin sheet metal skin might work well instead, especially if the edges are folded down over the front edge of the surface and secured to top braces. Such a skin could also be folded up at the back to prevent tiny screws and auto parts from falling into the cracks or seams commonly found on wooden surfaces. Check with metal suppliers and fabricators to see what is available and how much a custom skin would cost.

Many different materials are available for workbench tops, from rather soft, smooth fiberboard to vinyl sheets and laminates to galvanized sheet metal. You must first determine what kind of service you expect to get out of a surface material, and then talk to countertop professionals to see what is available. Look in the yellow pages under the heading of *Counter Tops*.

Additions

Any number of items could be added to workbenches to make them more versatile. Pegboard and hooks are great for hanging small tools and an assortment of supplies. A chalkboard may come in handy for drawing out specific metal fabrication plans and for listing specific tasks that need to be completed before an engine is ready for installation. Small desk lamps are handy for improving visibility while working on small assemblies, while a light mounted on an adjustable arm and equipped with a magnifying lens could really be handy for intricate work.

Every workbench should have at least one vise. A large, heavy-duty vise is needed for work on big auto parts, and medium vises work well for general pro-

At least one workbench in every automotive workshop should be outfitted with a heavy-duty vise. Along with the ability to hold items in a steady and secure position, vises are normally fitted with mini-anvils at the rear. Mounting bolts must be secured into sturdy workbench frame mem- *bers for optimum stability. The ends of workbenches are generally the most convenient sites for vises. In this location, users can take advantage of full workbench lengths to support work, and are afforded two workbench sides from which to work.*

In addition to workbenches, don't forget about counters and other table-like work centers. A counter like this one in Jack Holden's Champion Import Service makes a convenient place to research auto manuals, look through parts catalogs, and eat lunch, especially when furnished with comfortable stools. A similar tall counter may also prove useful for repair or restoration work on small assemblies and components that require close-up visual work.

jects. Soft vise pad inserts are available to gently hold delicate work, and small vises might fit the bill for procedures involving tiny auto components.

Another very handy workbench addition is an anvil. A chunk of railroad track will work well, as will a heavy piece of I-beam. These might be found at scrap yards or metal salvage/recycling facilities. Along that line, consider installing a piece of 1/4in or larger steel plate to a section of your workbench. A good size would extend from the front to the back of your workbench surface, and be about 3ft or 4ft long. It could be used as a small welding station, metal fabrication area, or a solid base for any other hot work or pounding.

A bench grinder is useful for all kinds of jobs. One equipped with both a grinding wheel and wire brush is great for removing rough edges from metal castings and for brightening oxidized metal parts. What about a buffing motor, bending brake, roller, and so on?

The types of work expected to be undertaken in a shop should offer plenty of ideas as to the kind of implements which would best serve workbenches. Auto body repair requires certain things that would not generally fit within the scope of engine rebuilding tasks. On the other hand, if you expect to complete a variety of automotive jobs in your shop, you might plan to outfit different workbenches with separate arrangements of related equipment and accessories, all located close to the shop areas where you plan to conduct those activities.

CHAPTER 7

WORKSHOP STORAGE

Workbench shelves will provide some storage. Large tools and equipment could fit on lower shelves, while smaller hand tools and some supplies might store well inside cupboards or on shelves located above. However, extra storage space should be allotted for other things like new auto parts, old ones awaiting restoration, car care products, lubrication supplies, maintenance materials, and a host of other shop necessities.

If your shop is designed as a two-story structure, consider turning the area under the stairs into a small storage closet. Attic spaces with strong ceiling joists

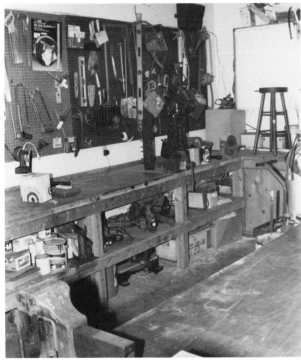

A major concern of any automotive workshop is storage. Along with auto parts, fasteners, paint products, and other supplies, tools and equipment must be organized in some fashion so they are readily available when needed. Pegboard and hooks provide a simple means for storing many hand tools, equipment accessories, and related items, while shelves and open areas under workbenches offer space for labeled boxes of auto parts and some workshop equipment. In lieu of open storage, consider the installation of cabinets with doors above workbenches, and the addition of doors to cover storage areas under workbenches.

About one third of Garry Allen's shop includes a second floor loft, which provides a small office area and large auto parts storage space. Because the ceiling height below this loft is shorter than that of the rest of the shop, the first floor work area under it is designated as a Concours preparation space—where the need to raise vehicles on lifts is negligible.

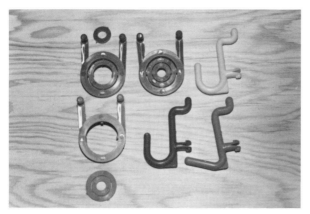

Standard metal pegboard hooks are notorious for pulling out and falling every time a tool or item is removed from them. This inconvenient feature of an otherwise handy means of tool storage is no longer a problem with the use of Sta-Put Color Pegs. These pegboard hooks are outfitted with a special protrusion which snaps through a second pegboard hole to hold hooks tight against pegboard. Designed for use with 1/4in thick pegboard, the hooks will hold up to 8lbs. Along with angle and round hooks, circular tool hooks with adjustable snap-out inserts are available in different colors.

might prove useful for storing some auto body parts during long-term restoration projects, as well as those shop items used only on rare occasions, like portable paint booth curtains, spare fluorescent light tubes, and so on.

Ideally, ceiling joists exposed at attic floor levels should be outfitted with 3/4in plywood runners to provide a solid storage base and serve as a walking or crawling surface. Without a base, only 1-1/2in joist edges can support any weight, as the spaces between them are covered only on the bottom with a ceiling's drywall. If you should step inside spaces between ceiling joists, your foot will go through drywall, unless you completely lose your balance and simply fall right through the ceiling and down to the shop floor.

If you prefer to have shop accessories out in the open for easy access, check out the variety of heavy-duty hooks, open shelving units, and other storage systems commonly sold at hardware stores and home improvement centers. By all means, talk with fellow auto enthusiasts and car club members to learn how they have mastered shop storage concerns. Some of their ideas could be altered slightly to fit right in with your needs and your shop's dimensions.

Although Garry Allen's Jags Plus is a professional business which sells auto parts to customers, there is no reason why home-based workshop storage areas cannot look like this. Simple racks with organized storage offer a quick and easy means for retrieving parts, supplies, and repair materials. Adequate lighting and a dust-free location away from active shop operations greatly help to make such areas efficient storage depots.

Basic Storage Ideas

It would be great to have a separate parts and inventory warehouse attached to your shop, especially one filled to capacity with row after row of usable stuff. Unfortunately, this kind of addition is far removed from the realistic budgets of most auto enthusiasts. In lieu of separate warehouse supply wings, owners of automotive workshops use their imaginations to devise methods that take advantage of every square foot of free shop space. Some have attached brackets to ceilings for the storage of long trim pieces, lengths of angle iron and other metal, straight tubing, spare light tubes, and so on. Others have built 12in wide shelves between ceilings and garage doors for small boxes filled with miscellaneous auto parts.

The kinds of things kept in your shop will greatly determine the type of storage required. Nuts, bolts, washers, and other fasteners should be maintained in segregated containers for quick and easy access. Various storage units are made for just this purpose. Some are in the form of small cabinets with lots of little clear plastic drawers, while others feature large drawers equipped with dividers. Professional auto body shops frequently utilize large metal cabinets outfitted with heavy-duty drawers divided into numerous individual storage cubicles.

Almost any type of fastener storage system beats a shelf full of old coffee cans loaded with a myriad of items of all different sizes, threads, and styles. New fastener storage units can be found in hardware stores, lumber yards, and most do-it-yourself home improvement centers. Likewise, shop around at swap meets, flea markets, and garage sales. *Hemmings Motor News* and other monthly auto publications frequently include advertisements and some reviews of

Heavy-duty fastener storage systems are available through companies which manufacture and distribute nuts, bolts, screws, washers, and related items. Home-based auto projects may not always warrant such large quantities of fasteners, nor the cost involved for the purchase of a similar storage system. However, you may find used parts bins like these at local auto swap meets, auctions, surplus stores, and business liquidators.

One tool box filled with clamps and metalworking hand tools not only keeps related items stored together for organization, it provides a quick and convenient way to bring all necessary items to an autobody repair area in one step. Likewise, an organized system of fastener storage, with removable boxes or trays, allows users to bring plenty of required nuts, bolts, washers, or related items to workshop spaces. Maintain specific types and sizes of fasteners in segregated containers, so their retrieval is easy.

unique fastener storage systems available through mail order. If you would prefer to build your own units instead of buying them, display ads with photos of storage products and systems may be clear enough to help you design similar storage bin components.

Lockers and Racks

Large metal lockers, like those in high schools, make ideal storage units, especially when outfitted with shelves that accommodate the specific heights of the items stored inside. Similar lockers could also be made out of wood. A 2x4 frame, covered with plywood and outfitted with either hinged or sliding doors, makes a nice locker for mops and brooms,

Metal lockers like these are very handy for auto workshop storage. Shelves are adjustable to accommodate numerous items, and doors help to keep dust and dirt out of the storage space. New lockers of this and other designs are available through hardware stores, some lumber yards, tool outlets, and industrial supply houses. Used lockers might be found at swap meets, surplus stores, and salvage yards, as well as large commercial buildings and schools scheduled for remodelling.

Adjustable open metal racks are familiar sights in the warehouse areas of auto parts stores and other commercial and retail facilities. They are designed to stand alone or be bolted to walls for added support. Heavy storage items should be placed on lower shelves and lightweight objects above to keep shelves from becoming top-heavy and prone to tipping over. Shelf systems like this are available through many of the same vendors that carry metal storage lockers. Likewise, look for used units through newspaper and weekly shopper ads or at swap meets and surplus stores.

coveralls, creepers, detailing supplies, paint masking materials, and the like.

Open racks may be fine for enclosed closet areas, but items stored on them will soon be covered with dust if they are simply left exposed in an open shop. Long, multi-shelf metal racks, like those commonly found in warehouse sections of auto parts stores, may also be found at surplus stores, business liquidators, hardware stores, lumber yards, and do-it-yourself home improvement centers. Light to medium storage racks can also be made out of wood. 2x4s are used for uprights and cross members, and then 3/4in plywood is used to make actual shelves.

Small shelving units are easy to make entirely out of 3/4in plywood. Cut plywood lengthwise into five pieces, each about 9-1/2in wide; this allows around 1/2in extra to account for saw blade cutting waste. Then cut pieces to length according to the height and length of your rack. Use drywall screws or large finishing nails to secure shelves to the side pieces. The top shelf should be a little longer than the rest so it can lay flat on both side units instead of being nailed between them.

New storage racks and shelf units are frequently sold at do-it-yourself home improvement centers and hardware stores. Costs range from under $20 to over $100, depending upon style and design. Used storage units might be found through the classified ads. Along with learning about various kinds of building materials and supplies sold locally through these ads, plan to attend auctions and other sales events held at gasoline service stations or other commercial/industrial buildings where businesses are liquidating inventory and fixtures.

Wood shelves are easy to construct using 3/4in plywood. Stand-alone units should be outfitted with a 1/4in plywood or fiberboard back panel to keep them square and stable. Wall shelves require that a section of wood be secured to the rear, lower part of shelves, which is then screwed or bolted to wall studs. For maximum strength, plywood should be cut and used so that its grain runs from one shelf side to the other, not from back to front. Since plywood sheets are 4ft wide, plan your shelf widths in such a way that minimal plywood waste occurs; do not forget to account for the saw blade's cutting width. These shelves are 9-1/2in wide. Five of them 8ft long can be cut from one sheet of plywood (five times 9-1/2in = 47-1/2in, with 1/2in allowed for saw blade kerfs). Secure shelves to sides with 3in finishing nails and wood glue. Use shorter nails for 1/4in back panels.

Dan Mycon uses a combination of open metal shelves and small cabinets for the storage of detailing supplies. Along with polishing products, he stores buffing pads, window cleaner, non-silicone dressing products, and cleaning supplies in these units located next to a large bay door. Just outside the door is an area used for auto washing, making this detailing supply storage location very convenient. Along with providing storage shelves and cabinets in your workshop, plan to fill them with items that will most commonly be used at their locations.

Cabinets and Cupboards

Shelves and racks are storage units without doors. Put doors on and they will most likely be called cabinets or cupboards. Although most dictionaries classify cabinets and cupboards as basically identical things, cabinets are often much deeper than cupboards.

Regardless of definitions, cabinets and cupboards serve as excellent storage places for tools, equipment, supplies, parts, manuals, and so on. Additionally, cabinets and cupboards protect items from dust, dirt, lint, overspray, and the roving eyes of thieves. Except for the additional work required to outfit basic shelves and racks with doors, about the only drawback to them is their concealing nature. Unless you place inventory lists on the doors, you will have to either memorize where everything is kept, or expect to open a few to eventually find what you are looking for.

Cabinet doors are made in a variety of styles, and outfitted with specific hinges to accommodate those designs. Doors may simply close onto the face of cabinets, or edges of doors could be cut down so half of the doors' thickness fits inside the opening, while the remaining, wider half makes contact with a cabinet frame face. In either case, basic shelf frames are faced with 1in wide boards along their tops, bottoms, and every side which will form the actual opening for doors. Just look at the cabinets and cupboards in your house to get a perspective on how basic ones are built.

Sliding door installations are another useful means for keeping dust and dirt off of stored items. Handy sliding door hardware kits in a variety of sizes are available at most hardware stores and similar re-

One way to increase storage capacity for hand and small power tools is to add on to an existing rolling tool chest. Snap-on offers a number of additions for their tool storage units, like this End Cab. Its drawers are 27in wide and 15-1/8in deep. It also offers a handy, 20x29in top work table. Snap-on.

Metal storage cabinets with locking handles provide secure places for expensive tools, auto parts, and other valuable items. They also make excellent storage units for supplies of shop towels, clean coveralls, respirators, dust masks, and other things you want to keep clean.

tail outlets. An advantage of sliding doors, as opposed to hinged models, is that they do not have to be pulled out and away from shelves in order to open. This feature might be ideal in places without a lot of extra room for swinging doors. A minor disadvantage of sliders is that one entire sliding door will always be in the way, either partially or fully closed, whereas hinged doors can both be opened wide at the same time.

Auto Parts Storage

At any given time during a full-blown auto restoration, chances are that an assortment of body, engine, and interior parts may be dismantled and in various stages of rejuvenation. A full-sized, two-car garage may find one stall filled with the project car and the other with dismantled and replacement parts. An important key in the successful completion of such projects, therefore, is an orderly system of parts storage.

Many small boxes with lids work well for securing related parts and assemblies together. Properly labeled boxes make parts retrieval much easier. In some situations, a number of small boxes could be placed inside a large box for easy storage in an attic or on a shelf—again, with the contents clearly labeled. This kind of system may be fine for small assemblies like lights, engine accessories, door panel hardware, instrumentation, and similar components, but what about the big items like fenders, grilles, bumpers, doors, and so on?

If your shop is big enough, a portion of it could be clearly designated for parts storage only. Large wooden racks with 2x4s standing upright could be made to support big auto parts like hoods and doors. Extra wide and deep shelves, measuring around 4ft by 8ft and made with 4x4s, 2x6s, and 3/4in or thicker plywood, may be just right for supporting windshields, fenders, trunk lids, tires, bumpers, and the like.

Finding places to conveniently store large auto parts is a concern shared by almost every auto enthusiast. Dismantled parts must be placed away from active repair areas so they do not hinder or obstruct work. Heavy-duty racks made of 2x4 or 2x6 lumber, secured to wall studs with long lag bolts, is one way to temporarily store auto parts like tires. You could design, build, and install a wider series of racks for doors, hoods, trunk lids, and other parts that can be laid flat across wood braces. Be sure all braces are securely held together with lag bolts or large nut-and-bolt combinations.*

The spacing between each shelf should be determined by the types of parts you expect to store. Provide a wide opening, about 3ft from the bottom shelf to the next, for heavy and awkwardly shaped parts like engines and transmissions. The second shelf could be placed at about the 4ft, 5-1/2in level to allow a full 3ft opening below and the top shelf to be positioned at around 6ft, 6in. The more narrow opening for the second shelf should be fine for slipping in doors, hoods, and other relatively flat parts, while the very top shelf might be ideal for bumpers, grilles, engine compartment aprons, and other parts that are slimmer and weigh less than doors and hoods.

Of course you can alter the dimensions of this extra heavy-duty rack to fit your specific needs. However, do not expect smaller lumber to hold up to the weight amassed by the disassembly of an entire car or truck. Plan on using 4x4 legs, 2x6 long braces, single 2x6 cross braces 16in on-center, 3/4in or thicker plywood, long lag bolts with washers for the frame, and 10d nails for the plywood. A 4ft by 8ft, extra heavy-duty auto parts storage rack of this kind will require the following materials:

—six 4x4s at 8ft for legs;
—six 2x6s at 8ft for long braces;
—seven 2x6s at 12ft for the shorter 4ft cross braces;
—thirty-six 3in by 3/8in lag bolts and washers to secure the long braces to the legs (two each);
—three 4x8ft sheets of 3/4in or thicker plywood; and
—four pounds of 16d nails to secure cross braces.

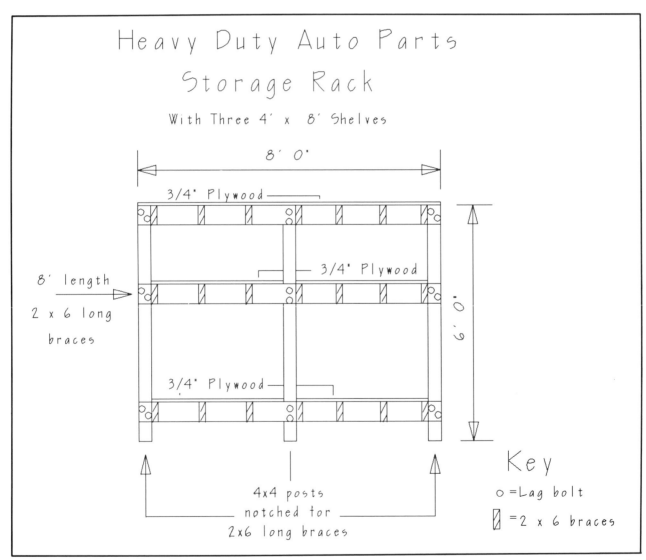

This is a simple design for a three-shelf, heavy-duty, auto parts storage rack constructed with a 4x4 and 2x6 lumber frame and 3/4in plywood shelves. Shelf spacing can be adjusted as desired, as can the unit's overall dimensions. Basically, 4x4 posts are notched on the outside face for 2x6 braces. 2x6 cross supports are then placed and secured to the braces 16in on-center with 16d nails or lag bolts. Plywood is then placed over the braces to offer three 4ft by 8ft shelves.

The following directions—and accompanying drawing—describe how to assemble the storage rack: Be sure your 2x6s measure exactly 8ft long, the length of plywood sheets. On each 4x4 leg, mark the locations where each long 2x6 brace will be attached. Be sure to mark the the 2x6 board's entire 5-1/2in width because you are going to notch each 4x4 so that the brace will fit flush on the 4x4. Set the depth of your circular saw to 1-1/2in, the true thickness of a 2x6 board, and run your saw numerous times through the area to be notched so that you end up with a series of very thin strips of wood. Use a hammer and chisel to clean out the notches. 2x6 long braces will fit into these notches and be secured with lag bolts.

Once the first long 2x6 braces have been lag-bolted to the 4x4 legs, cut the 12ft 2x6s into 3ft 9in boards. They will be placed between the long 2x6 braces to serve as front-to-back cross braces. Since you will want this unit to be a full 4ft deep, cross braces must be cut at 3ft 9in to account for the depth taken up by the long braces—one long brace front and one rear accounts for a total board thickness of 3in (two times 1-1/2in equals 3in). The leftmost, middle, and rightmost cross members will be nailed to the 4x4 legs and long braces. Each of the others will be placed at 16in on-center.

Once the unit has been nailed together, notch two plywood sheets to fit between the 4x4 legs. Slip them into place and nail securely. The top plywood shelf should not have to be notched. This new, extra heavy-duty auto parts rack will now offer you a total of 96sq-ft of solid storage.

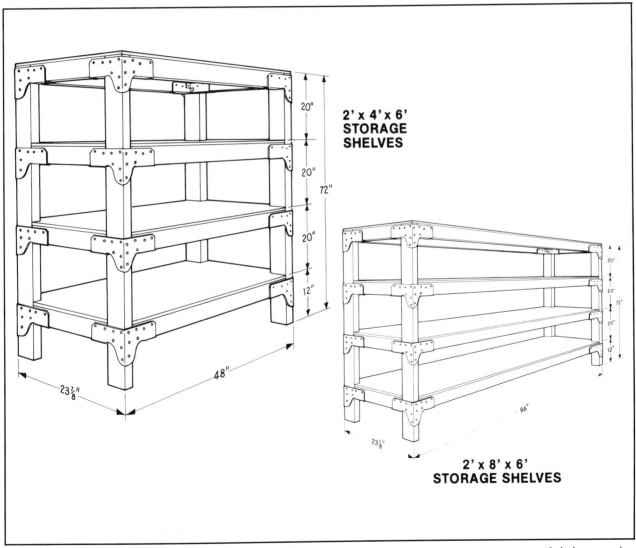

2' x 4' x 6' STORAGE SHELVES

20"
20"
72"
20"
12"
48"
23⅛"

2' x 8' x 6' STORAGE SHELVES

20"
20"
72"
20"
12"
96"
23⅛"

Rigid Tie Corner Connectors from the Simpson Strong-Tie Company make it easy to design and build a sturdy storage unit. When constructing a long unit be sure to install cross braces 2ft on-center, or 16in on-center if shelves are destined to support exceptionally heavy loads.

A system of small drawers supported by a frame and shelves is ideal for the storage of small parts, especially those that have been restored and must remain idle until the rest of an automobile's restoration has been completed. Drawers that contain fragile parts like gauges, highly polished interior accessories, and other such pieces could be lined with rubber mats or thick, soft, cotton. Drawers like these are also handy for the storage of wiring looms, hoses, light bulbs, and so on.

Although it appears that these berry bushes are about to devour Bill Snyder's small storage shed, the structure provides a place where large autobody parts can be stored out of the weather until he is ready to restore them. Sheds and other outbuildings may serve as inexpensive auto workshop storage additions, especially for those who may have more than one project vehicle dismantled in their shop at any given time.

John Roberts is always looking for good deals on 1955–1957 Chevy parts. He may not always need particular pieces at the time they are purchased, but he figures he will some day. To accommodate the safe storage of these parts, he built a small enclosure onto the back of his shop, one which extends from the eaves to a short wall and is covered with panels of opaque fiberglass. He also installed a large, lightweight metal roof that runs from the eaves at the back of his house to the eaves at the front of his shop, creating additional storage space which offers protection against rain and snow.

Special Parts Storage

There may come a time when you need a special storage facility for restored parts that must wait months before a host automobile is ready for their installation. Since these parts must be carefully stored to prevent accidental damage, a means must be provided for their safety. If a dedicated storage facility is not available, and your shop's attic space is not a viable option, you may have to come up with something a bit out of the ordinary.

Would a small, separate storage building behind your shop serve the purpose? Some small metal storage sheds can be purchased new for as little as $130. Used ones might be found in classified advertisements for a lot less. Small storage sheds made out of wood are also sold through independent dealers and large retail chain stores. They cost more than $200, with prices going higher for larger models. What about a self-serve storage facility? One-car garage size and smaller units generally rent for around $40 per month.

If none of those storage ideas meets with your approval, and your shop just doesn't have a separate safe storage area, then consider building a strong wooden box for special parts, much like crates used by professional household moving and storage companies. You may even be able to purchase large used crates from moving, storage, or freight hauling companies. Since such a crate will be strong, it could double as a work table in a corner of your shop, providing it is equipped with a solid plywood top that prevents dust or liquids from entering.

Wood pallets are common sights around many commercial and retail centers; a few of these nailed together could make a semi-solid border around parts, with a heavy car cover added for extra protection.

Delicate items, like restored antique gauges, knobs, and trim pieces, should not be simply tossed into a cardboard box for storage. If yours is an active shop, consider nailing a few boards together into a box and then lining it with soft cotton material to protect pristine parts from crushing and scratches.

Storing special auto parts may require some brainstorming to be safely preserved while minimizing the shop space taken up in the process.

To complement the storage shelves and cabinets in your workshop, consider using conveniently sized tool boxes to hold related items together in a single, organized package. Like a tool chest filled with wrenches, ratchets, and sockets, separate tool boxes could store specifically related items like engine diagnostic and metering equipment, pinstriping and paint touch-up utensils, clamps, electric system supplies, and so on. Tool box units also help to prevent large storage shelves and cabinets from becoming cluttered with lots of small, separate items scattered about.

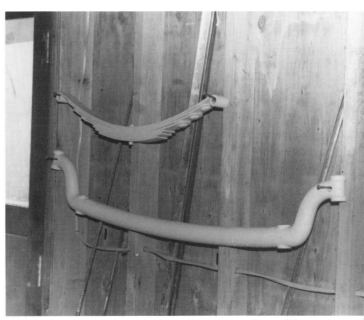

Because so much of his time is spent at Newlook Autobody and on hot rod projects, it is taking Bill Snyder a lot longer than expected to fully outfit and set up an adequate storage system in his auto workshop. In the interim, he has found a safe way to store some restored suspension parts by hanging them on wall studs with sturdy nails. This means of parts storage may not be preferred, but it keeps parts protected from nicks and scratches by getting them off of the floor and out of the way of other restoration activities.

Flammable Materials Storage

Almost every automotive workshop contains some flammable liquid product. Lacquer thinner, paint thinner, reducers, solvents, and gasoline are most common. Whenever a flammable liquid is used for any auto repair or restoration endeavor, all potential sources of ignition must be turned off completely or totally eliminated. Such might be natural gas or electric water heaters, wood stoves, space heaters, boilers, electric motors, hot plates, microwave ovens, and lit cigarettes.

When not in use, flammable liquids should be stored in sealed containers and, preferably, inside flammable liquid storage cabinets. Professional auto shops are required to keep all flammable liquids in approved cabinets. Paint shops and other facilities which keep large supplies of flammable liquids on hand are required to go a step further and provide special storage rooms. These rooms include heavy, fire-retardant walls and doors, a berm around their perimeter to confine spills, and even a fire sprinkler head installed in the ceiling.

Active auto enthusiasts with just a few gallons of thinner, reducer, or other flammable liquid on hand do not have to spend a lot of money installing an approved safety store room. However, they should have a separate cabinet set aside for just the storage of flammable liquids. This cabinet should be as far away as possible from heaters, wood stoves, and other ignition sources. In fact, it would be a good idea to place

Flammable liquids like lacquer thinner, paint reducers, and other petroleum-based products should be safely stored away from all potential sources of ignition. Flammable liquid storage cabinets are made of metal, and fitted with tight-closing doors. They are available at many autobody and paint supply stores and safety supply outlets. If you plan to stock more than a couple of gallons of flammable liquid in your auto workshop, seriously consider the purchase of a similar storage cabinet that will help improve your shop's overall safety.

Professional autobody paint shops are frequently required by building and fire departments to install flammable liquid storage rooms for the safe maintenance of flammable paint products. Along with fireproof walls and fire doors, these units feature concrete berms around their floor perimeters, designed to contain spills. They are also outfitted with explosion-proof lights, and many are required to have a fire sprinkler system. All paint supplies are stored in this room at Newlook Autobody. All paint mixing operations are conducted in it, as well.

flammable liquid storage units against an exterior wall and close to a large door. You may even consider installing a screened vent on the exterior wall behind a cabinet, to allow fresh air to keep that space well ventilated.

Because gasoline is such an volatile material, you are highly encouraged to confine gasoline storage to the outdoors. If need be, build a small shelter, like a shed for garden tools, that includes a safe and well-ventilated space for gasoline storage.

All flammable liquids pose potential fire hazards. You must eliminate all ignition sources before using any of them. In addition, you must make their storage a serious concern. First off, all flammable liquids should be kept in metal containers with tight-fitting lids. These should then be stored in an area where they will not be knocked over or run into—ideally, in a corner next to a large bay door. A specific cabinet labeled for flammable liquids alone would serve to further protect these containers.

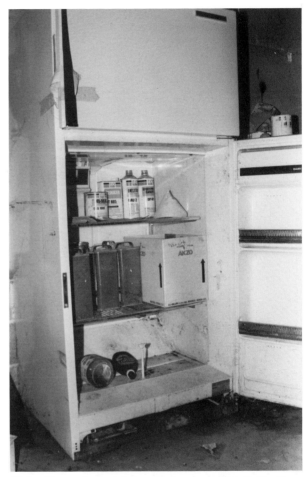

Gasoline is a very volatile and flammable liquid. It must always be stored in containers designed for gasoline, and should never be stored inside auto workshops. Instead, it should be stored outside in sheds, away from all possible ignition sources. A small garden tool shed with a large ventilation opening at the base is one safe storage location. Pouring spouts should be removed from gasoline cans as soon as they are no longer being used, and replaced with tight-fitting caps. Excellent gasoline storage cans feature spring-loaded caps that always remain sealed except when being used.

Old refrigerators and freezers may serve as suitable flammable liquid storage units as long as their tight-fitting door seals are intact. The seals help to confine flammable vapors and prevent them from escaping into workshop spaces where they may come in contact with ignition sources. Be certain that all containers are stored upright, with their tight-fitting lids properly sealed.

CHAPTER 8

SPECIAL BOOTHS

For automotive repair and restoration purposes, a booth is generally defined as something that helps to confine the atmospheric pollution or other operational effects of certain procedures within protective barriers. Likewise, booths may also be designed to keep contaminants out of specific work areas.

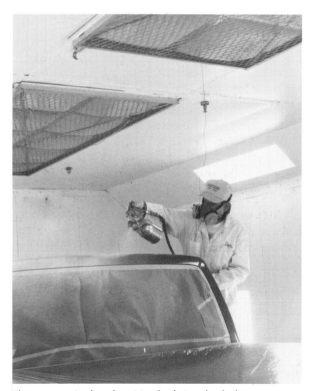

The spray paint booth at Newlook Autobody features a ventilation system which helps to keep contaminants out of the booth environment and also filters out paint overspray before it can be released to outside air. In addition, fluorescent lights are mounted outside the booth, separated from paint atmospheres by clear panels sealed with gaskets. Dan Mycon has installed wire hangers suspended from filter screens as a means to hold small parts so that their entire assemblies can be painted at one time. Notice that this spray paint booth is outfitted with a fire sprinkler system.

Spray paint booths are designed to keep contaminants out of work areas while minimizing paint product oversprays. Welding booths help to keep sparks confined to fireproof work areas and block wind currents that could disrupt MIG welding operations (arc welding with the enhancement of an inert gas that purifies immediate welding spots at the tip of a welding gun). These booths may also offer protection for bystanders by way of screens that block bright arc welding light.

Other booths are also common sights in many automotive workshops. A sandblasting booth helps confine media to specific work areas, as well as protect nearby objects from inadvertent blasting. Auto body sanding booths outfitted with large ventilation ducts work to remove clouds of sanding residue from work areas and prevent these clouds from infiltrating other shop spaces. Large shops might include auto detailing booths, separate areas where clean cars and trucks are detailed to maximum perfection without worry of sanding dust, sandblast media, or other debris.

A personal automotive workshop may not require a fancy paint or detailing booth because those activities will probably be the only ones underway when undertaken. A person working alone can only do one thing at a time. However, the installation of specific booths might go a long way toward helping to keep your shop area clean, safe, and efficient. To learn more about specialty automotive booths, talk to fellow auto aficionados and read through auto magazines which frequently offer special workshop sections with tips and ideas from readers.

Spray Paint Booth

Paint booths are probably the most widely talked about shop area in the fields of auto body repair and restoration. This is likely due to the stringent environments paint booths must maintain in order for painters to produce top-quality work. A speck of lint or wind-blown debris would easily mar an otherwise perfect paint finish, which is one reason why high-tech professional paint shops insist upon installing state-of-the-art downdraft paint booths in their shops. Costs for these paint booths can easily exceed $100,000.

Another reason many professional paint shops are installing expensive paint booths is to conform with rigid governmental regulations that limit the amount of paint overspray that can be emitted into the open atmosphere. Air quality has become a major issue all over the country, and overspray filtering and removal systems installed as part of these new-age spray paint booths are designed to eliminate most overspray, if not all of it.

Professional paint booths are also designed to maintain clean atmospheres. Paint shops need these because their regular work areas produce a great deal of dust from sanding and metal repair. If a shop were kept meticulously clean and the government didn't require filtering systems, paint shops might not need special paint booths. This should support the idea that enthusiasts can build makeshift paint booths that prevent contamination of paint finishes. All that is needed is a clean environment free from wind currents, as well as plenty of good light and a reliable air pressure source.

Mike Holiman has successfully painted many vehicles in his shop. He installed a cable next to the ceiling that runs around the perimeter of an entire vehicle bay. A thick piece of heavy-duty plastic is outfitted with grommets through which regular shower curtain hooks are inserted. Hooks are placed over the cable to suspend a plastic curtain, and within minutes a portable spray paint booth is ready to go. A powerful squirrel cage fan is mounted on an exterior wall close to the ceiling as a means to exhaust paint overspray. Its suction power is so great that Holiman has to hold nearby booth plastic out of the way with bungee cords. To ensure maximum dust control, he wets the floor and gravel driveway just outside thoroughly.

A portable paint booth similar to Holiman's can be made in your shop using basically the same materials. In lieu of a cable, grommets, and shower curtain

This large squirrel cage fan in Mike Holiman's auto workshop does an outstanding job of removing paint overspray. A cable stretched around a stall (next to the fan's support brackets) supports a large curtain made from heavy-duty plastic sheets. The curtain's top edge is outfitted with grommets through which standard shower curtain hooks are inserted. These hooks are placed over the cable to provide a suitable workshop painting area. Bungee cords are used to secure the paint booth curtain around the perimeter of the squirrel cage fan inlet.

Although not nearly as sturdy or convenient as Holiman's portable spray paint booth, a makeshift paint booth can be made from sheets of heavy duty plastic secured to ceilings and floors with lath and tape. Plastic top edges are rolled around lath strips that are then nailed to ceiling joists. Bottom plastic edges are secured to the floor with strong duct tape. Be sure plastic is positioned away from light fixtures, as their heat could cause plastic to melt.

hooks, you could use a more lightweight plastic, and duct tape—although a problem with duct tape is its tendency to leave globs of glue and tape on surfaces. Two-inch wide automotive masking tape will not leave any residue, but plastic must be quite lightweight in order for this tape to hold it up securely. Tape should also be used to secure plastic to the floor

Large fans are very useful during spray paint work. They help to remove clouds of overspray, and also bring in fresh air. This fan is located high on a wall, next to the ceiling. It should be complemented with another fan located on the same wall but placed closer to the floor, to help remove overspray hovering at floor level. In addition, consider installing a fan on an opposite wall to draw fresh air into the shop from outdoors. Position it high enough so that dirt and debris are not sucked in from surrounding flower beds or landscaped areas.

so it will not blow around as air pressure from a paint gun is deployed.

The ceiling above any portable paint booth must be free from dust, cob webs, and other debris. Ideally, it should be covered with drywall and properly painted. If your shop's ceiling features open joists and rafters, consider covering it with plastic. Cut or secure plastic away from light fixtures. Heat from them could cause plastic to melt or catch fire.

Air ventilation must be accounted for in any portable paint booth. Holiman's squirrel cage fan draws overspray away from the paint area and helps to bring fresh air over the curtain from a large bay door directly across from the fan. This works great as long as dust and debris are not sucked in through the door—another major reason why Holiman wets down the driveway before painting. If you do not have a fan system for your shop, plan to use portable fans at both the front and back of your booth to keep air moving. Plastic can be taped to fan cages to prevent it from being sucked into the blades.

The air flow from one fan should direct fresh air into the booth area, while the other should be placed in a position to draw air out of the booth. To help reduce the introduction of dust and debris into the area, tape a section of clean cloth over the cage of the fan that is supposed to bring in fresh air. The material should be lightweight and free of lint, like a clean bed sheet.

Another way to ventilate portable paint booths is with attic fans. Large cfm attic fans are designed to replace hot, stagnate attic air with fresh air pulled in from eaves vents. You could install one or two such fans in your shop's attic and run ducting from them directly to the ceiling above the portable paint booth stall. Be sure an on/off switch is provided for fans, as many of them normally operate from thermostat controls. For maximum safety, install fan motors away from potentially flammable overspray.

The advent of catalyst hardeners for automotive paints has greatly enhanced the durability of modern paint finishes. Urethane paint products feature the best qualities of enamels with the ability to cover in just a couple of coats. They also offer the best qualities of lacquers by allowing nibs to be sanded smooth and repainted within very short time frames. However, urethane paints do have a distinct disadvantage in that their hardeners contain isocyanate materials. These substances are very harmful to human respiratory systems, and every auto paint manufacturer highly recommends that all users wear positive pressure respirators.

Sandblasting Booths

Some do-it-yourself auto enthusiasts prefer to sandblast outdoors so that clouds of media and debris can blow away in the breeze. However, the introduction of affordable sandblast cabinets has greatly reduced the need to sandblast outside.

Large sandblast candidates, like frames, will not fit into cabinets. Unless some other facility is available, they have to be sandblasted in a shop or out on a driveway. On a rainy day or one filled with snow, your options are pretty much limited to the shop. In these cases, consider erecting a portable booth similar to the ones described for painting. Heavy shower curtains, or sections of thick plastic secured to the ceiling and taped to the shop floor, should do a good job of keeping media confined.

Your portable sandblasting booth will work best when plastic is sealed tightly to the ceiling with plenty of 2in automotive masking tape. Use lots of tape at floor level, too. Clouds of sandblasting dust will rise and flow over the top edges of curtains to finally settle on everything in your shop if curtains are not tightly secured.

Although the air inside sandblasting booths will not be filled with isocyanates, it will be heavily polluted with dust. Therefore, be sure to wear a quality respirator under your sandblast hood. A section of plastic should be left open at the door to your shop to allow the introduction of fresh air. Be sure plastic is secured around the door edges. Enlist the help of attic fans and squirrel cage fans to keep air moving and assist in the removal of dust clouds.

Sandblast cabinets are great shop accessories, especially for those who enjoy restoring old cars that may suffer rust and oxidation problems on many of their small- to medium-sized parts. A wide variety of

A sandblast cabinet does an excellent job of confining sandblasting activities to just a small area. For the most part, media is maintained inside the unit, with only small amounts of dust escaping when cabinet doors are opened. Sandblast cabinets are equipped with heavy-duty rubber gloves, suction tubes, and nozzle assemblies. Media is recycled through a bottom siphon for repeated use.

A portable sandblasting or welding booth is easy to construct out of plywood. Quite simply, nail two, three, or four sheets together at their corners to make an enclosure which will help to confine sandblast media or welding sparks within its borders. Clouds of sandblast dust may flow over short enclosures, but could be curtailed with sheets of plastic draped from the ceiling to plywood. Along with confining media, a portable booth like this will prevent accidental blasting of cars, workbenches, and other items close to the work area. In the case of welding, the enclosure blocks blinding arc welding light from others in the shop.

sandblast cabinets is available, from small, inexpensive units that use your compressor for an air supply, to large, costly, stand-alone, self-contained units.

Because media is confined to the interior of sandblast cabinets, nearly all concerns over dust control are eliminated. Users do not have to wear uncomfortable and rather hot safety hoods, either. These handy units feature a reservoir where media is recycled over and over again, which not only makes for clean sandblasting but helps to save money, too. Expect small to medium units that can easily fit on top of workbenches to cost around $325. Optional accessories include interior lights, stands, vacuum systems, and swivel wheel kits. Larger ones that stand alone start at about $700 and continue higher as more options are added to the package. Such options may include an air compressor, vacuum system, sandblast tips, and an assortment of media.

Welding Booth

As mentioned earlier, a welding booth may serve several important safety functions, like keeping sparks away from combustible materials and protecting bystanders' eyes from bright arc-welding light. In addition, a small welding booth is very handy. How many times have you wanted to quickly weld a small section together but dreaded the thought of having to pull your welder out of its cabinet, hook it up, prepare a welding spot, find clamps, and so on? Well, a welding booth already set up and outfitted with all necessary tools should quickly get rid of those dreaded thoughts.

Mike Holiman does a lot of welding on top of a 1/4in sheet of steel plate mounted on a workbench. You could build a separate unit with a fireplace brick floor and walls made of 16-gauge or thicker metal. Be certain the brick and mortar used are designed for

Sandblasting cabinets are available in different sizes and with various extras. Small units easily fit on top of workbenches, while larger models stand alone on their own support frames. Options include interior cabinet lights, vacuum systems, and foot controls. This bench top model offers a 24x24in door opening and 24x12in window. This sandblast cabinet requires a compressed air supply of 7cfm at 80psi. The Eastwood Company.

high temperatures. A facility 3–4ft wide and 30–36in deep should offer plenty of working room. Wall heights of 24–30in should be sufficient. Although some enthusiasts have encountered good results with a sand base for welding booths, fireplace bricks will offer a much cleaner working environment.

Along with plenty of clamps and welding rod, be sure your welding hood, gloves, apron, and respirator are kept close to your welding booth. This way they will always be on hand when you need them. Plan to install a fan somewhere close to your booth, with a duct that runs to a hood over the welding area. Include a bright light over the work area, too. A curtain made from heavy material will help to keep blinding arc welding light out of other people's eyes while you weld. Attach a small cable to the ceiling with hooks. Then put grommets along the top edge of your curtain, and insert shower curtain hooks through them.

If you need a welding booth much larger than one built on top of a workbench, consider using hinges to fasten two or three sheets of 1/2in plywood together. They can be unfolded to offer a portable set of walls that will keep sparks confined and shield others from bright arc welds. Use heavy-duty hinges with quality screws, nuts, and lock washers.

In order for three sheets to fold together tightly and neatly, you will need to cut about 2in off of one sheet's edge. This strip will be used to block up the third sheet as it is folded down on top of the other two. With two sheets flat on the floor, envision the one on the right with 2in cut off of its right side. That strip is attached to the far left side of the sheet on the left. After they are both secured with hinges, fold the one on the right on top of the one on the left. It should slip in next to the 2in strip.

Now, lay a third sheet down to the left, next to the 2in strip. Hinge the third sheet to the 2in strip and then fold it on top of the other sheets. They should all fit tightly together in a neat stack. To use this portable booth, simply stand up the sheets of plywood and unfold them. Sheets of plywood could be cut down to more manageable sizes if desired. You might even improve on this idea and build a portable plywood partition with four sides. Cut 2in off of the fourth sheet's far edge and attach it on top of the 2in strip already in place. Hinge the third sheet on top of this second 2in strip. Then hinge the fourth sheet to the open edge of the third sheet. The fourth sheet will fold on top of the third sheet, and then they will both be folded over on top of the first two at the same time.

Partitions

Sometimes, the work you need to accomplish in one part of your shop is not compatible with something else occurring in another—grinding and metalwork, for example, taking place next to a vehicle recently prepared for a car show. In this case, a partition between vehicles would prevent accidental spark damage or inadvertent blows from the back of a bumping hammer.

A simple way to separate two areas is with sliding doors, like those on clothes closets. Track hardware is readily available at hardware stores and do-it-yourself home centers. Partitions can be made with plywood, drywall, discarded closet doors, or any such panel material.

Drywall might be good for those shops with tall ceilings, as it comes in 8ft, 10ft, and 12ft lengths, all 4ft wide. It is available in 1/2in and 5/8in thicknesses. Before using drywall as a partition suspended from a track mounted to the ceiling, you will have to reinforce its top edges with strips of wood on both sides. Hold the strips tightly together with sturdy screws placed on 2in centers. Drywall is very heavy and its composition will not support its suspended weight unless reinforced.

Portable partitions could also be made out of

Because Mike Holiman completes a lot of small welding projects on top of a large piece of steel plate attached to a workbench, he stores welding rods nearby in a metal cabinet. The unit is outfitted with dividers to separate different-sized welding rods. An illuminated light bulb inside the enclosure does an excellent job of keeping the welding rod dry during damp weather.

wood, with wide-based wheels at the bottom as opposed to being suspended from ceiling tracks. Individual units could be rolled around anywhere in a shop as needed. About the only drawback to these are their rather unstable nature: A stiff breeze could knock them over. Therefore, be sure portable partitions are outfitted with wheels that extend at least 6–8in on both sides.

Overview

The basic objective in providing special booth areas inside automotive workshops is to keep contaminants either in or out of specific, confined spaces. A further advantage is the opportunity to keep all related tools and equipment at specific spots for convenience and efficiency. Keep these thoughts foremost in your mind as you design your shop, and spend plenty of time with graph paper, pencil, and 1/4in scale ruler, drawing in various floor plans until you arrive at the one which appears to best accommodate the majority of your needs. Along with that, plan ahead for future shop additions.

Two, three, or five years down the road, you may be in a financial position which enables you to add a wing onto your shop. If you planned ahead from the outset, this wing might clearly fill specific needs by joining up with existing designs to offer a perfect sand-

blasting or welding area or a separate paint booth. It might even afford you an individual facility designed strictly for detailing a show car or Concours d'Elegance preparation. Outfitted with hot and cold running water, a floor drain, lifts, and lots of maneuvering room, while separated from all of the dirty work frequently associated with auto repairs and restoration, this area could complement the rest of your shop by easily providing you with a place to fine-tune your restoration efforts into best-of-show results.

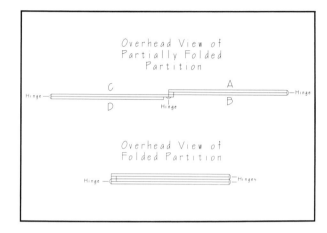

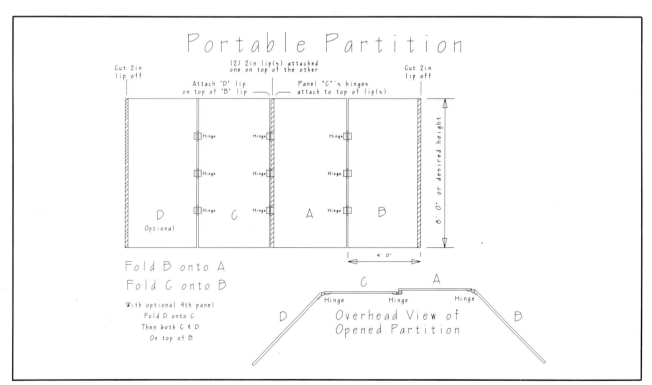

A portable partition can be made out of plywood and hinges. Plywood panels may be cut to any size desired to accommodate various needs. However, lips must be cut off outer panels and then installed on the inside edge of an inner panel, to allow panels the ability to fold together flat.

An extra-large partition, made with full 4ft by 8ft sheets of 3/4in plywood, will be too heavy for one person to carry. Consider building large panel partitions with lighter, 1/2in plywood.

CHAPTER 9

PITS AND LIFTS

An automotive workshop pit or lift will greatly ease work on vehicle undercarriages. Mechanics frequently raise automobiles with floor jacks and support them on top of sturdy jack stands to access undercarriage units for repair or restoration. Although sufficient room is generally made in this manner, anyone who has ever experienced these cramped environments will attest to the awkwardness of having to work on one's back while struggling to move heavy parts in very confined spaces. Pits and lifts offer means by which people can stand and more easily maneuver beneath vehicles.

Basically, pits are rectangular holes located in the middle of workshop parking stalls that mechanics climb into for easy access to undercarriage areas. Lifts are mechanical units used to raise and support vehicles high enough off of the ground that mechanics can walk and work under them.

Pits must be dug out, have reinforced concrete walls and a floor installed, and be outfitted with lights, a stairway or ladder, and a very strong, secure lid that will cover the hole and support the weight of vehicles driven over. Lifts are simply installed on a shop floor, secured with anchors, and equipped with power. Unless you have experience building strong retaining walls, you will probably have to hire a building contractor to install a pit. Although crews are generally available to install most lifts, many two- and four-post models are advertised as units that can be erected by purchasers who closely follow assembly instructions.

Pits Versus Lifts

Industrial strength metal concrete subfloor forms allow actual concrete workshop floors to be poured directly over basement areas. This gives a brand new meaning to the term *work pit*. Today, ambitious auto enthusiasts have the option of constructing viable basement workshops under their regular shop facilities to not only double floor space but take advantage of pit assets without the restraints of narrow concrete pit walls.

This is a state-of-the-art automotive work pit at the Minit-Lube oil change shop in Kirkland, Washington. In reality, it is much more than a simple work pit, as the lower area is part of a complete basement. For many years, auto enthusiasts regarded standard narrow auto work pits as features which made oil changes, chassis lubrication, and some undercarriage work much more convenient. With the advent of special metal floor supports onto which concrete shop floors are poured, enthusiasts with the means now have the option of constructing extra-large pit work areas that surround main floor pit openings.

Understandably, the cost to construct a work pit the size of a basement may be quite high. However, the advantages are enormous. Transmission work, parts storage, and lots of other endeavors could take place there. A basement floor would certainly support heavy loads, and large items could be lowered into and raised out of this space by way of come-alongs, block and tackle units, or motorized cable lifts. When pits are not in use, heavy-duty lids could safely cover them. While the second floor of a two-story workshop would support the weight of some light to medium storage and repair items, a basement could essentially serve as a complete second shop facility when outfitted with a car lift that reaches the main floor level.

Looking down through a pit opening from the mainfloor workshop, you will notice a long, wide shelf used for tool storage. Beneath that is a supply of oil filters. Although this pit facility has been outfitted for a specific business, auto enthusiasts who construct similar structures could store tools and equipment relevant to their needs.

This is a section of metal sub-floor, on top of which a concrete floor has been poured. Structural members like this enable builders to construct complete basements under automotive workshops. A building engineer or architect will have to draw specific plans to ensure structural support is complete throughout. Additional support, by way of concrete and steel columns, may be needed under auto lifts located on mainfloor workshops.

Plenty of room is available for storage in the basement area under the mainfloor shop. Lights and shelves are plentiful. A full-sized basement, outfitted to serve the needs of an auto enthusiast, could be set up to accommodate the rebuilding of engines, transmissions, and a host of other assemblies. Heavy objects could be lowered and raised through pit openings by way of come-alongs, blocks and tackle, or motorized cable lifts.

Although full workshop basements are possible options, overall costs for construction may cause many enthusiasts to gear down their expectations and settle for much smaller, so-called "regular" work pits that measure around 3–4ft wide, 16–24ft long, and 5–6ft deep. Here is where the design and limited usability of these pits initiate debates among professionals and enthusiasts. With regard to the cost of construction as it relates to the amount of actual work that can be accomplished, many feel that money earmarked for such pits would be much better spent on more versatile and useful two- or four-post, above-ground lifts.

Mike Putnam regards normal work pits as virtually worthless when compared to lifts. He says, "Pits may be fine for changing oil and chassis lubrications, but it's impossible for two guys to maneuver around in one while pulling out a transmission." He praises the design of two- and four-post lifts that allows full access to vehicle undercarriages.

With one post located on each side of a vehicle parking stall, two-post lifts feature twin arms that extend from each post to balanced lifting points under automobiles. An electric/hydraulic system provides the power to raise cars, and specific safety features physically lock lifts into position. Four-post lifts incor-

Auto work pits equipped with drains make periodic cleaning easier. Building Departments may require such drains to have sumps or other features that will collect petroleum products and other pollutants before they reach main sewer systems. Environmental rules and regulations regarding waste water and other runoff have become quite stringent in recent years, so be sure to gain building department approval before making such installations.

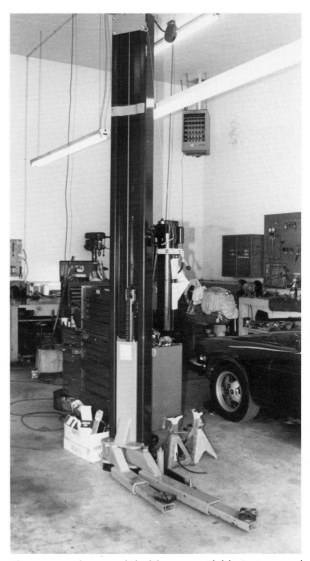

Above-ground automobile lifts are available in two- and four-post designs. This is one part of a two-post lift. Notice that lifting supports swing out of the work area so that vehicles can be driven into the space without going over them. These lifts are designed to support vehicles at different heights to accommodate various auto repair and restoration efforts.

porate posts at all four corners of a parking stall, with ramps that vehicles are driven onto. A similar electric/hydraulic system is responsible for raising units, and physically operated safety locks keep lifts in raised positions to negate any possibility that a power loss would result in their indiscriminate lowering.

Although it appears that the advantages of a post-lift may far outweigh those of a single-stall pit, you must decide which option can best serve your needs. While designing your new shop or contemplating the addition of either a pit or lift to your existing shop, be sure to fully investigate and compare the actual costs for both types of installations. Labor and material for the construction of pits will vary widely throughout the country. In addition, building codes may not allow the installation of pits in your area, or the position of existing plumbing beneath your shop site may make such an addition impossible to accommodate. Conversely, since post lifts are erected completely above ground, there should be no restrictions or obstructions to prevent their installation.

A number of companies sell two- and four-post lifts that vary in price, size, weight capacity, and height. Advertisements for these companies are commonly found in automotive periodicals such as *Hemmings Motor News*. Prices generally start at around $2,500 for minimum-capacity lifts, and climb higher for units capable of lifting greater weights.

Work Pit Designs

Basic work pits can be no wider than the inside distance between the wheels on any vehicle serviced. This generally limits pit width to about 3ft. Pit length should be sufficient to service vehicles while having an additional extension to serve as an emergency escape route. In other words, if a pit 16ft long is required to maximize accessibility to all vehicles to be serviced, then build a pit 20ft or 24ft long so that you will have an unobstructed exit in case of a fire or other emergency.

Naturally, a ladder or set of steps will be needed at one end of the pit for access. This space will al-

Post lift designs incorporate arms or ramps that do not block access to undercarriage assemblies like transmissions, differentials, and suspension members. As opposed to center column lifts, post lifts afford plenty of working room around vehicle underbodies because posts are located off to the vehicles' sides. As seen here, virtually every part of a vehicle's undercarriage is accessible. Positive mechanical locking devices prevent these lifts from lowering due to power outages, hydraulic or pneumatic leaks, or other such situations.

ways be open because you need a way to enter the pit after you have parked a vehicle over it. An emergency escape route must be located at the other end so that you can safely exit either direction without delay. If a pit were designed with a single entrance at the front, for example, and you were at the back when a fire broke out between you and the front exit, how would you escape if there were no rear emergency exit? In addition to front and back steps, some pits feature stairs that exit to the sides to areas between stalls. These require heavy-duty bridges across them to support vehicles driven over the pit site.

The depth of your pit should accommodate your height. Although 5–6ft is common, you may want to make yours deeper dependant upon your height. Optimally, you should not have to duck your head or stoop while working on cars from inside pits. A pit that is too deep can be outfitted with a wooden deck to raise its working level. However, one that is too short will require its existing floor be jackhammered out, dug deeper, and then replaced with a new one—an expensive, labor-intensive, and needless waste of time and money. To determine your most comfortable working depth, visit a place that already has a

Here you can see up through the pit opening and across a portion of the Minit-Lube basement area. Notice that a heavy-duty pit cover is outfitted with rollers so that it can quickly and easily be maneuvered into place to completely cover the pit opening. Hand tools and supplies are readily available for technicians working under vehicles.

More than one exit should be provided out of every auto workshop basement. This safety precaution gives people in basement areas two escape options in case of fires or other catastrophes. One set of stairs could lead to the mainfloor workshop, and another might lead to an outdoor exit.

pit and ask to inspect it. Bring a tape measure along to determine exact dimensions. Add or subtract to that pit's depth to accommodate your needs.

Forming and pouring concrete pit walls will require the expertise of a professional concrete contractor. Concrete is very heavy, and the forms designed to hold it all together must be securely constructed. In addition, excavation activities will require that constant shoring devices be installed and/or adjusted to maintain adequate protection against the potential of a cave-in or wall collapse. Although you may be able to complete some of the pit installation yourself, you are highly encouraged to seek the assistance of a professional to ensure proper pit installation. A vehicle's heavy weight is perched close to the edge of the pit and will cause stress on its walls. This must be accounted for in every design so that adequate reinforcement is provided.

The actual hole will have to be dug at least 1ft longer and 1ft wider, maybe more, to allow for 6in or thicker concrete walls all around. It must also be dug at least 4in deeper to make room for a concrete floor. Your local building department should help you determine how much of which size rebar reinforcement is needed and how it should be secured to the adjacent floor. Do not forget to run an electrical line to the pit to power lights, and at least one outlet for power tools. An air line and drain are also excellent accessories.

Ron Weglin points out a significant safety concern regarding the accumulation of carbon monoxide inside work pits. Carbon monoxide is heavier than air and tends to seek low points in which to settle. The exhaust from vehicles near pits could fill pit areas with dangerous carbon monoxide gas thus endangering pit users. Carbon monoxide is odorless and tasteless. Those affected by it will get lightheaded and sleepy, and soon pass out. If not rushed to a hospital, those afflicted with carbon monoxide poisoning will die. Therefore, plan to install a ventilation system in your pit to keep potentially lethal gases out and plenty of fresh air in.

Pits must be outfitted with strong, removable lids so they can be securely covered when not in use. Left open, pits are a very dangerous hazard. In order to keep shop floor areas intact, some enthusiasts have built a series of three or four separate, heavy-duty wooden lids that fit over wide (4in or more) lips along entire pit perimeters. Each section is very strong so it can support the weight of vehicles driven on it. Car decking lumber (tongue and groove 2x6 material), reinforced with 2x6 braces beneath, should be considered an absolute minimum for this function.

Check with your city's building department to learn of specific code guidelines affecting this type of building application. In addition to wooden pit covers, you should investigate the availability of heavy, rolling metal lids; heavy iron grates; and other suitable pit cover options.

In addition to standard pits that run lengthwise along vehicle stalls, you may have an interest in outfitting your shop with other kinds of versatile pits. Some front-end alignment specialty shops install shallow pits at the front of alignment ramps that allow technicians to sit on caster-equipped stools and simply roll from one wheel to the next. Front-end pits range from 3–4ft deep, depending upon a technician's height and the type of casters and stool used. Width should be ample to allow maneuvering around both the front and rear sections of front suspensions—anywhere from 3–5ft, depending upon your preference.

Shops install different sized pits to accommodate their specific needs and desires Visit a few shops equipped with different pits to get an accurate idea of which design and dimensions may best suit your needs. Talk with technicians, too. They may have innovative suggestions that could help you design a more comfortable and efficient pit.

Automotive Lifts

Just about everyone who owns a car is familiar with automobile lifting devices. They have seen them in gasoline service stations, general auto repair bays, and dealership service departments. Although first thoughts of installing a lift in your shop may be exciting, you must contemplate a number of options and drawbacks before purchasing one.

Standard, single-column center lifts can be inexpensive if acquired from gas stations or other auto repair shops that are going out of business or planning for complete renovation. Initially, they might appear to be excellent bargains. However, because of increasing environmental restrictions regarding underground leaks of all kinds, installation of these units may require strict adherence to stringent and expensive guidelines. This is due to the fact that the columns go into the ground, and many contain hydraulic fluid which could leak and then leach into surrounding soils.

Along with that concern, the actual installation of such a lift might be beyond your skill level, requiring you to hire a professional construction company. The fees for installing a lift, properly securing it, and providing a power supply must be added onto the unit's initial cost. Considering those factors, along with the fact that a center lift will most likely block access to the middle of vehicle undercarriages, you might decide that the advantages of two- and four-post, aboveground lifts may be well worth any extra money.

Some favorable characteristics of two- and four-post lifts have already been mentioned. But positive comments continue to come from many professional auto service technicians. Garry Allen believes his post lift is an excellent shop addition, and could not imagine getting by without it. Putnam wishes that each of his mechanics had two of them to work from. While one supported a vehicle in repair limbo, another car or truck could be positioned on the second lift, and his mechanic could get right to work.

Both Ron and Rick Weglin say that their lift was the best piece of equipment they have ever purchased for use in their shop. Since their lift positively and completely locks in the fully raised position, Rick says they have no worries about leaving a car parked on it up in the air, pulling another auto into the space beneath, and conducting repair work on the lower vehicle. He does suggest, however, that an inexpensive shower curtain or wide sheet of plastic be placed on the lower car to protect its finish against inadvertent fluid leaks or debris that may fall from the upper car. Another advantage is the ability of lifts to raise and secure vehicles at specific heights to accommodate any repair endeavors.

As with any lift, you must be concerned about ceiling height and actual lifting space. Many post lifts are designed for areas with low ceilings, and may work fine for small- to medium-sized vehicles and full-sized convertibles. Information about dimensions, capacities, and prices are readily available through lift manufacturers. They will also furnish specific information about required base surfaces and preparing areas for lift installations. You are encouraged to contact a number of lift suppliers to receive their informational packages. Compare the benefits and prices of each model and select the one which best suits your needs, shop size, and budget.

Two- and four-post lifts are capable of lifting vehicles high enough that another one can be driven underneath, as seen here. This feature may not always be a priority for auto workshop owners, but it is a handy option when one vehicle is torn down while on the lift and another needs just a few simple repairs at the same time. Ron and Rick Weglin have utilized this parking system numerous times. Draping an inexpensive shower curtain over cars parked under those on lifts will prevent oil leaks or other debris from marring paint finishes.

Automotive post lift installations are not confined to workshop floor areas. Some models can be erected outdoors where vehicles are frequently steam-cleaned or where they receive undercarriage baths. A two- or four-post lift may be an ideal accessory for large carports built off of workshops where cars may be parked one above the other.

Ramps

Lifts and quality heavy-duty jack stands should be the only items you ever trust to support a raised automobile while you are under it. NEVER rely on *any* type of jacking equipment alone to support vehicles while anyone is under them for any reason. Every jack is susceptible to failure and may cause heavy vehicles to drop, potentially trapping or crushing anyone underneath.

For conveniently and quickly raising vehicles slightly off of the ground to accommodate oil changes, snow chain applications, undercarriage inspections, and other tasks, however, consider the use of heavy-duty ramps. Commercial ramps made of metal are frequently sold at auto parts stores and some tool outlets. They are generally capable of supporting autos about 10–12in off of the ground. This may allow just enough room for you to gain access to oil pan plugs, speedometer cable connections, park-

This is one of two identical, handy ramps, made to accommodate the installation of snow chains during winter. Depending upon the normal undercarriage clearance of vehicles parked on this ramp, the few inches of lift it provides may be just enough to accommodate oil changes, lube jobs, parking brake adjustments, and other maintenance tasks. Be sure to securely block those wheels not parked on ramps to prevent vehicles from rolling off of them.

ing brake adjusters, and a host of other quick maintenance items. Whenever using ramps, be sure the wheels still in contact with the ground are securely blocked to prevent vehicle movement.

In lieu of store-bought ramps, you can make some out of lumber. 2x10 lumber is actually 9-1/2in wide, sufficient to support most common tire sizes. Purchase two 2x10s 10ft long to make ramps that will raise vehicles 6in off the ground. Mark boards at 1ft, 3ft, and 6ft intervals. Use a saw to cut each board at the prescribed marks. You should end up with four sections from each board, for a total of: two pieces measuring 1ft long; two at 2ft; two at 3ft; and two at 4ft. Set your saw at a 45 degree cutting angle and then cut one end of each board down to a 45 degree angle. The angle makes it easier for tires to roll up onto the boards.

Lay a 4ft board flat on the floor, with the 45 degree angle sloping up. Place a 3ft board on top of it so the square end is flush with the 4ft board's square end. This board's 45 degree angle must also slope up. Nail them together with 16d nails driven in at an angle so they do not exit the bottom of the 4ft board. Next, lay the 2ft board on top of the 3ft section, nail it, and then put on and nail the 1ft piece. Attach an adequate stop at the end of the top board to prevent tires from going too far forward on the ramp. A minimal stop would measure no less than 2in wide and 2in high. Complete the same procedure for the remaining boards and you will quickly have assembled a set of handy, heavy-duty ramps.

Similar ramps may be constructed out of wider boards for vehicles that sport oversize tires. Although 6in is quite high for homemade ramps, you could opt to purchase another 10ft board of equal width, cut it into two equal 5ft pieces, add them to the bottoms of the 4ft boards, and increase your ramp's height to 7-1/2in.

General Pit, Lift, and Ramp Safety

No personal injury has ever helped to hasten the completion of any auto work. Injuries cause lost work time and may result in large hospital bills. Working under heavy automobiles from pits or units raised in the air puts people in precarious positions. Your escape options are few if a car should fall on top of you because of improperly set safety devices or haphazard ramp usage. After squeezing under a low-slung car to get into a pit, could you exit fast enough to escape injury if a fire broke out?

These are serious concerns that must be contemplated every time an automobile is positioned for repair work. Fire department, rescue squad, and ambulance record books from across the country include incidents where professional and do-it-yourself auto technicians have become trapped, seriously injured, or killed as a result of vehicles falling or catching fire during repair. Do not allow yourself to become a similar statistic through haste or negligence.

ALWAYS follow common sense and recommended safety practices whenever raising, supporting, or working under automobiles. Block tires, double-check safety locks, enter pits through wide open entrances that are clearly marked so bystanders do not fall into them, cover pits immediately after use, install fire extinguishers in pits and close to lifts, hang brightly colored ties from low-lying parts on cars raised on lifts, and take the extra steps every time to ensure safety practices are followed religiously.

As you place greater emphasis on your own safety needs and practices, don't be surprised if your efforts are noticed by others, especially younger family members new to the interesting world of automotive work. Your safety-consciousness should be a positive example to newcomers so that they, too, will enjoy a lifetime of injury-free automotive enthusiasm.

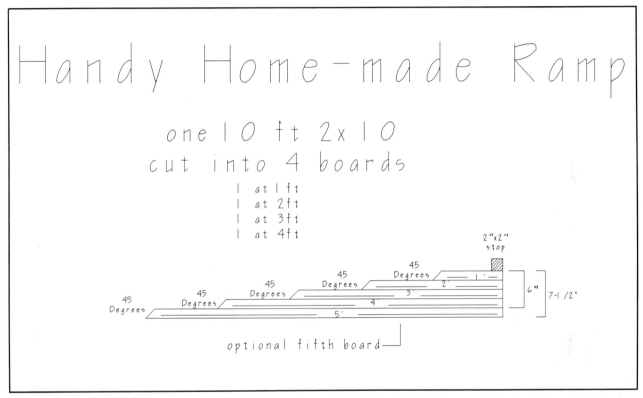

A set of handy auto ramps can be made out of two 10ft, 2x10 boards. Purchase a third 10ft 2x10, and the ramps' *lifting capability is increased by an additional 1-1/2in for a total lifting height of 7-1/2in.*

CHAPTER 10

AUTOMOTIVE WORKPLACE EXTRAS

This is a compact bender manufactured by Lockdown Securities, Inc. It is capable of bending metal stock in all sorts of shapes, as illustrated here. An instruction booklet clearly shows how to make specific bends with different sizes of metal. The unit must be securely anchored to the floor with sturdy bolts. This might serve as an efficient piece of equipment for auto workshops, especially those where lots of custom autobody work is undertaken. Lockdown Securities.

Jack Holden's auto repair garage is set up just the way he likes it. He and his mechanics enjoy an organized shop, with tools and equipment conveniently placed around efficient workbenches and lifts. To ensure a clean atmosphere, a commercial vehicle exhaust system is set up with tubes at each work stall. A section of this exhaust tubing is suspended by a spring-loaded ratchet cable reel, which is pulled down when needed or left out of the way when not. A vacuum and duct system pulls vehicle exhaust through tubes to a central vent.

Together with owning a few very special, one-of-a-kind automobiles, winning a couple of lotteries, and being crowned Best of Show, auto enthusiasts dream of having a workshop dedicated to repairing, restoring, and maintaining cars, trucks, and other motorized equipment. So far, this book has suggested many ideas on how to design, build, and outfit such a facility. This chapter will enhance that information by expounding on many little details that could truly turn otherwise-ordinary workshops into very convenient and comfortable work places for both you and your vehicles.

In essence, automotive workshops are rather generic buildings with typical building conveniences like running water, heat, walls, a roof, and a floor. What makes them special to people who enjoy automobiles is the fact that they are filled with things that help make vehicles look, smell, feel, and run better than ever before. Tools and equipment are mandatory items without which auto care would be difficult to accomplish. Although, these instruments are the backbone of any automotive workshop, it is the creature comforts, handy gadgets, innovative step-savers, and unique shop accessories that make workshops personal.

You will undoubtedly spend a lot of time in your new or remodeled workshop, and that time should be well spent. Of course, you'll be intent upon accomplishing a lot of work while in there, but workshops should also be fun places where enthusiasts can unwind from hectic work days, tinker with projects, and teach offspring and others the ins and outs of automotive work.

In addition to planning and designing storage systems and other workshop accessories, do not overlook simple conveniences, like this seat on wheels. Casters make these rolling chairs very maneuverable, and the handy shelf below the seat is perfect for tools, fasteners, and small parts. Similar seats are available through many auto parts stores, tool outlets, and mail-order businesses.

Quick-Grip clamps are excellent shop accessories. Dan Mycon is using two of them to hold down a fender while he does some hammer and dolly work on a few dents. Quick-Grips are available in a number of different sizes. They are lightweight, secure quickly, and are easy to maneuver.

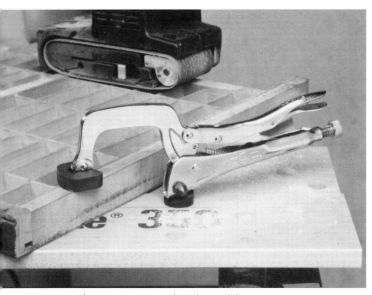

Clamps are essential tools used for many automotive repair and restoration endeavors. They are commonly used to secure items for welding, cutting, and polishing, and a long list of other tasks. This is a new type of Vise-Grip, hold-down clamp, specifically designed for use on drill presses with holes for clamp attachments. American Tool Companies, Inc.

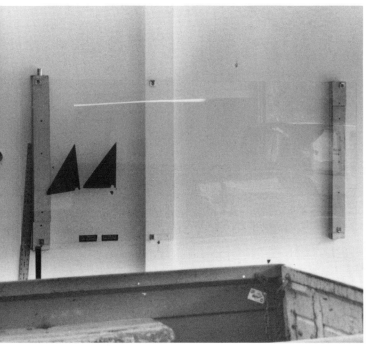

To assist his efforts while installing window tint, Roy Dunn installed a simple piece of plexiglass on top of a couple of pieces of wood. Two wing window tint strips are currently attached to the unit. This small item works as both a tint film holding accessory and cutting board. Little shop conveniences like this can turn otherwise generic shops into personalized ones.

Beyond the information in this chapter you are encouraged to read auto-related periodicals, especially those which feature sections on new tools, equipment, and devices that could help to make your projects progress faster and with fewer head-scratching sessions. Those magazines which feature reader write-in hints, like *Skinned Knuckles* and *Sport Truck*, frequently offer suggestions so simple and ingenious that one can only say, "Now, why didn't I think of that?!"

Vehicle Anchoring Devices

How many times have you wished there was a way to solidly anchor an old sled so that you could tug here or pull there to straighten a bumper, frame member, or other rigid component? Well, a few holes drilled in your concrete floor and filled with chain link anchor-ties are just the answer. Commonly available at auto body and supply stores, these items hold fast while great pressure is applied against them. No more chaining bumpers or frames to trees or telephone poles.

Concrete coring companies have special equipment that can quickly drill holes in concrete. Chain link anchor-ties fit into these holes and remain virtually unnoticeable until needed. Just pull the cap off and the chain is readily available for you to attach come-alongs, frame straighteners, hydraulic pulls, and so on. If your auto body and supply store does not carry these items as part of its regular inventory, you can bet that it has a supplier just a telephone call away. Along with installing anchors at all four corners of work stalls, read information about the specific kinds of frame-straightening devices you will be using to learn where additional anchors should be located.

Utility Workbenches

When starting out on a repair project, most semi-knowledgeable enthusiasts grab a handful or two of the tools they expect will be needed for the duration of a specific repair session. Veterans spend more time contemplating Murphy's Law, and bring extra tools and materials to designated work areas. Still, it seems even those extras are seldom enough for the task at hand.

To avoid frustration, consider setting up one or more portable carts loaded with all of the items most often needed for particular repair operations. One cart could be supplied with auto body repair tools and materials; another with clamp assortments, copper paddles, a grinder, spare grinding disks, and other welding equipment; another with paint masking supplies; and so on. This way, you can be assured that the majority of items for specific tasks will be at hand when you need them. As you gain more experience working with designated carts, you will become more familiar with those items which always seem to be missing or running low, and can improve that inven-

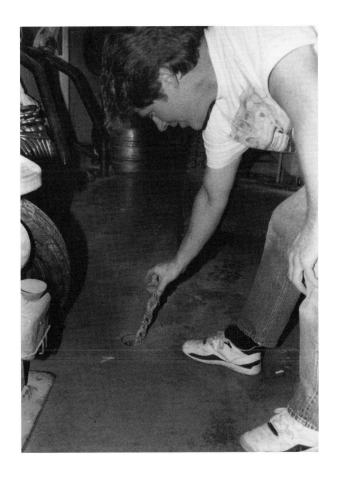

Personal safety around automotive workshops must be practiced at all times. Never hesitate to don a dust mask, gloves, and a full face shield whenever working with grinders, sanders, buffing machines, and other power equipment. A full face shield will not only protect your eyes but will also prevent sharp pieces of metal from becoming embedded in your face. When working in dusty conditions, plan to wear a dust mask to protect your respiratory system from airborne contaminants. The Eastwood Company.

Major autobody repairs frequently require that great pressure be applied to frame members and other body assemblies to pull out twisted metal or line up components that were forced out of position. Expensive frame straightening machines incorporate their own anchoring devices, but you can install this type of floor anchor at a fraction of the cost. A concrete coring company must be called out to drill holes in your shop floor so that anchors can be installed. Once in place, a metal lid will cover holes and also serve as a means to retrieve chain, as John Roberts demonstrates. Hooks on working chains or cables are placed over links on anchor chains for rock-solid stability. These devices are generally sold at autobody paint and supply stores.

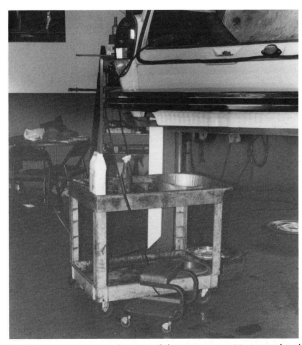

Rolling carts serve as very useful step-savers. You can load them with tools, parts, and supplies and then roll them to the shop site where you plan to conduct specific work. Enthusiasts have outfitted similar carts with pegboard and hooks to hold wrenches, screwdrivers, and other hand tools. Large hooks may be just right for securing air hoses or electrical extension cords. Cart wheels should be large enough to handle the weight placed on them. Wheel locking mechanisms are also handy accessories, especially when working on sloping driveways.

tory until you have a fool-proof system of quantity control.

If much of the auto work you delve into consists of one or two separate types of endeavors, one portable cart should support the bulk of your hand and power tool needs. If a small work table is a common requirement, purchase or build a cart which will haul your tools efficiently and provide a work space on top. For greater convenience, make sure your cart includes drawers, a storage cabinet, pegboard sides, and other features

A couple of small drawers at the top of such a cart could hold screwdrivers, nut drivers, ratchets, sockets, and the like, while a lower cabinet would store metering devices, battery-operated power equipment, replacement ignition parts, spare belts, and so on. One side equipped with pegboard and hooks might be handy for an assortment of combina-

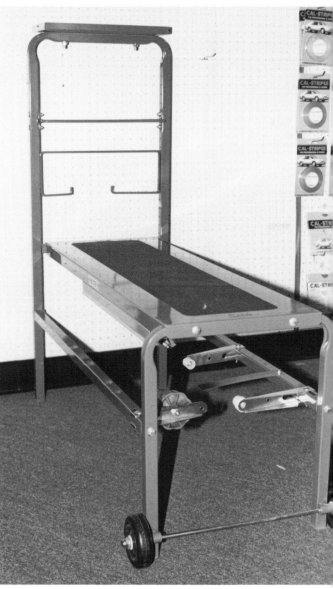

This workbench-on-wheels has been designed as a precision brake service station. Equipment attachments are stored under the work top on pegboard hooks. You could design and build similar rolling carts, outfitted with the tools and accessories most often required for specific tasks. A cart loaded with sanders, sandpaper discs, grinders and grinding discs, hammers, dollies, and metal cutting tools might serve autobody repair endeavors well. Another cart could be set up with masking paper, tape, and other tools used to assist in auto paint masking. Ultimately, you could set up a number of carts, each stocked with the regularly used supplies of the type of work it is designed to serve.

For those enthusiasts with avid interests in auto spray painting, masking paper and tape units like these may be worthwhile workshop accessories. Masking paper applications go a lot faster and smoother when masking tape is automatically applied by such devices. Autobody paint and supply stores generally carry an assortment of similar masking accessories.

tion wrenches. A couple of portable clamp lights hooked onto a cart lip would be handy, along with an extension cord neatly coiled around them.

The other side, outfitted with a set of small shelves, could hold air cleaners and other parts commonly removed during tune-ups. This will leave the cart top open as a tray for tools and replacement parts and for projects like cleaning and adjusting spark plug gaps. With such a cart, you would not have to constantly walk back and forth to a workbench for tools, parts, and so on.

Rick Weglin complains that his giant tool chest on wheels is just too big. The top is so far off of the ground that he has to stand on his tiptoes to see what is in it. He would much prefer a wheeled tool chest with a flat top at waist level so he could reach back while under a hood and set down parts and tools. This is the exact idea behind designated portable carts/workbenches on wheels.

Ron Weglin's regular tool chest stands almost 6ft high. This makes it difficult for him to see what is inside the top compartment and upper drawers. This height makes it inconvenient to reach tools while stretched out over an engine compartment adjusting a distributor or carburetor. To solve that problem, Ron purchased a shorter tool chest with an open work top. Now, he can place tools and replacement auto parts on the tool chest top, keeping them within easy reach during tune-up and repairs conducted under the hoods of cars and trucks.

The Smithy Company's drill mill lathe is a compact machine shop in itself. Set up on its own workbench, this piece of equipment has all of its attachments located close by, in drawers and on shelves. When someone needs to use the machine, all accessories are within easy reach to efficiently complement work efforts. The Smithy Company.

Small- to Medium-Sized Storage Containers

No true auto enthusiast worth his or her salt would ever throw away perfectly good screws, nuts, bolts, washers, wire connectors, sections of wire, rubber boots, springs, gaskets, tubes of sealer, knobs, bells, or whistles. "Someday, they will all come in handy," we say. This leaves us with something of a dilemma as to how and where to intelligently and categorically store all of these good and usable used parts.

Magazines that regularly feature reader shop hints frequently print advice about this exact dilemma. If your goal is a place to store unsorted hardware, that old standby the 3lb coffee can comes to mind. Another possibility is to cut a 45 degree angled opening in a spent rectangular gallon can at the top corner farthest away from the handle. Roll back cut metal to alleviate sharp edges. Once a month you should go through your accumulated, unsorted hardware and put washers with washers, bolts with bolts, and related items with their cousins in a more organized fastener storage bin.

For a short-term hardware container, lay an empty antifreeze container on its side and then cut out most of the top panel. This unit will never tip over, can hold a lot of stuff, and makes parts-retrieval a snap. The same goes for empty, one gallon plastic milk containers and just about every other one gallon plastic jug. In fact, these can be cut to conform to virtually any need as long as it does not entail the use of lacquer thinner or any other potent liquid.

Old, worthless extension cords have been suggested as straps for screwdrivers, as have worn-out seat belts. Starting at one end drive a nail or screw through the cord or strap into a panel at the back of a workbench, make a loop through which a screwdriver could be fitted, and then drive in another nail. Repeat this until you have created enough loops to hold the desired number of tools. This thrifty means of converting an otherwise useless item into a convenient one is a tribute to the ingenuity of auto enthusiasts.

Heavy-duty plastic and wire milk crates designed to tightly fit atop one another are common sights around grocery and convenience stores and other places where milk is sold or warehoused. A contributor to *Skinned Knuckles* magazine suggests that an angle iron frame with casters, made to hold two to four such crates at the base level, makes an ideal used parts storage bin.

These crates can be stacked four or five high and filled with miscellaneous parts or tools that are easy to see because of the crates' grid construction. Casters enable units to be turned around for viewing, as well as moved to various shop locations as needed. When a desired part is spotted in one crate, those above it are easy to remove and replace. You can remove whatever items you want without compromising the balance or integrity of the unit, though you should try to avoid stacking heavily loaded crates on top of empty ones

Workbench drawers are very convenient storage areas. A problem with drawers, though, is that they frequently get so cluttered that it becomes difficult to recognize just what's in them. One option is to divide a drawer into cubicles by utilizing numerous 1/4in board sections. Or one could simply go to a variety

Ordinary plastic and wire milk crates make handy storage units for dismantled auto parts and many other loose shop items. They stack on top of each other to minimize the amount of floor space they take up, and they are easy to see into. Extra-small items like fasteners will fall through grid bases, so you will have to keep them stored in a small cardboard box or plastic bag with related auto parts in these containers.

store and purchase a number of kitchen silverware trays with separate slots already built within.

These items feature different sized slots that could accommodate many items. If they will not work for you, try a stationery store which carries a selection of drawer organizers designed for desks. Although they may be intended to separate paper clips and rubber bands, their design could be most useful for keeping nuts, bolts, washers, and electrical clips confined to individual parts of a workbench drawer.

Books, manuals, magazines, and other written works are extremely important to Concours competitors and serious restorers because they contain information on how to rejuvenate, set up, and properly outfit specific automotive assemblies according to original factory guidelines. Materials like these are invaluable. They have to be preserved for future reference because similar copies may never again be available.

They are also important to serious Concours competitors when it comes time to prove to judges that projects were completed according to factory specifications. Such proof can easily make the difference between Best of Show and third place.

In lieu of storing valuable manuals, booklets, pamphlets, newsletters, and other paperwork in drawers or scattered closets, purchase file cabinets and organize a systematic means of categorization. File cabinets could be located in office or research ar-eas, restroom facilities, parts storage sites, or other places where workshop sanding dust and other debris cannot infiltrate their drawers. If you are an avid Concours person or serious restorer, it would be wise to accumulate as much authentic written information as possible with regard to your automobile of interest. Authenticity is worth a great deal in both Concours point values and dollars. Enclose special papers and pamphlets inside plastic sheet protectors for maximum care.

Baby food jars with lids used to be favorite storage containers for various nuts, bolts, and small items of all kinds. The idea of nailing their lids to shelf bottoms and simply unscrewing jars for access was very good. However, glass breaks when it hits a hard surface, and it is also difficult to hold onto with greasy hands. Therefore, the use of plastic jars with lids appears to be a better alternative.

To complement your shop with a nifty fastener bin, simply build a rack of shallow shelves mounted close to a workbench. Then, outfit it with a series of equally sized plastic jars, screwing their lids to the bottom of the shelf above. Clear plastic jars offer excellent viewing, and their quick disconnection from lids makes it easy to retrieve items. If inclined, you could further organize this system by filling and labeling each jar with specific fastener items like lock washers, flat washers, metric nuts, American nuts, and so on.

Storage systems for small fasteners range from 3lb coffee cans to sophisticated displays like this. Available through Wickliffe Industries, Inc., these jars are clear, making it quick and easy for users to spot the fasteners needed at the *moment. Lids are equipped with hooks to keep them firmly secured to pegboard. Various size containers are available.* Wickliffe Industries, Inc.

Keep It Clean

Retail companies offer products designed to catch oil and grease drips before they stain shop floors. You can accomplish much the same goal by laying a sheet of heavy cardboard beneath vehicles and on top of sheets of plastic. Cardboard tends to absorb oil and grease to keep it from spreading, while plastic underneath prevents floor stains. Dan Mycon

A powerful vacuum capable of sucking up liquids as well as dry material should be considered a primary auto workshop accessory. Along with quickly cleaning off workbench tops and floor areas, a wet/dry vacuum can suck water and shampoo out of auto carpets after an interior detailing; pull dust, dirt, and debris out of nooks and crannies after an autobody sanding operation; and so on. This vacuum comes with two extension wands and a combination floor attachment that works on both wet and dry floors. The vacuum head is easily removed so that the 45 degree angled tube can be used for high volume water removal tasks.

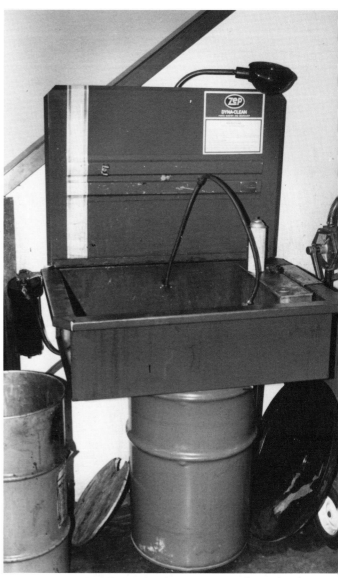

Parts washing tubs filled with solvent are normally outfitted with a fusible link device which automatically closes the lid if solvent in the tub catches fire. The aerosol spray can resting on the ledge of this parts washing tub would prevent the lid from closing completely. You must be certain that all safety devices throughout your automotive workshop are in satisfactory working order, and that other objects will not impede their ability to function in an emergency. In lieu of petroleum-based solvent parts washing tubs, investigate the availability of non-petroleum-based cleaning solutions which do not pose the threat of fire.

says that disposable baby diapers do much the same thing, but they are small and must be placed accurately in order to catch all drips and leak problems.

It is impossible to work on any automobile without experiencing dirty arms, hands, fingers, and fingernails. Most commercial hand cleaners do an excellent job of removing grease and grime. However, removing such debris from around fingernails is a problem. Many variety stores sell small plastic brushes designed for fingernail cleaning. They are gentle and yet do a good job, especially when combined with hand cleaner. Soft, used toothbrushes do a good job, too. Together with saving toothbrushes for auto detail tasks, keep one by your shop's slop sink for fingernail cleaning.

Empty 5–25gal drums can double as clean rag storage bins and stools. Plywood circles cut to fit just inside the tops of containers, with second circles cut a larger circumference to rest on their rims, could be glued together, outfitted with a pad, and covered with a strong seating material stapled to the bottom plywood lid.

Plastic shoe bags are designed to hang from clothes rods inside clothes closets. These clear plastic units feature numberous pockets into which shoes may be stored. Clear plastic shoe bag panels can also make great small auto parts storage bins. They are relatively strong, have decent-sized compartments, and are see-through, enabling you to clearly identify contents immediately. About the only drawback is that most styles are open at the top. This could allow normal shop dust to enter storage compartments, unless they are stored in closets, second floor storage areas, or other places away from regular shop activities.

After Dan Mycon installed this paper towel dispenser in his autobody shop, it quickly became one of its most useful and convenient accessories. In lieu of using clean shop towels for the removal of large globs of grease and grime from autobody parts, technicians employ paper towels and then throw them away. Paper towels are also quite useful for drying hands, removing oil leak drops, wiping off grease and grime from tools, and a host of other things.

Large cans work well for storing clean shop towels and rags. A lid prevents workshop dust and dirt from soiling them before they are used. Ten to 15gal cans seem to be a good size—not too big, but large enough to hold good quantities of supplies.

Shop Liquids

Used motor oil should not be dumped on the ground or poured into sewer systems; it should be recycled. Most people who change their cars' motor oil do not have any objections to recycling the used crude, but are sometimes at a loss to figure out reasonable ways of storing it until it can be brought to a recycling center. A 25gal storage drum would be handy, but how does one lift and transport such a heavy container? A pickup truck is needed, of course, along with a ramp that can be used to roll a full barrel onto the truck bed, or a hydraulic lift, like an engine hoist or truck-mounted mini-boom.

A more practical means for storing used motor oil is the use of smaller containers. One gallon plastic milk jugs (four quarts) make good waste oil receptacles. Two are generally needed to hold all of the oil from a typical engine. Although plastic milk jugs are outfitted with snap-on lids, the weakness of their structure could result in lids popping off should jugs be squeezed tightly together or knocked over.

In lieu of plastic milk jugs, consider heavy-duty 5gal plastic buckets. They are big enough to hold oil from at least four changes, equipped with sturdy carrying handles and tight-fitting snap-on lids, can be carried when full by one person, and will not take up much work shop space. Five gallon buckets can be found at bakeries, restaurants, and many other food service places. Alternatively, you might purchase laundry detergent in a 5gal bucket, and then use the empty one for used motor oil and other storage.

Used motor oil is recycled at Mathewson's Automotive & Tire. To accommodate used oil storage, a large holding tank was installed at the rear of the shop facility. It is pumped out on a regular basis by an oil recycling company. A metal roof was built over the tank to prevent water buildup inside the leak-confining berm around its base. Used oil filters drain into this tank through a box connected to the tank's filler tube. A raised grate at the bottom of the box allows oil to flow into the tank's tube.

Mike Holiman built this jib boom for less than $100 by purchasing the bulk of materials from a metal salvage yard. The most expensive items were tapered roller bearings used at both top and bottom support points. This unit will rotate 360 degrees, making it great for pulling engines and setting them on the heavy-duty table next to the work bay. To ensure that this jib boom would not cause any workshop structural problems, he poured a deep concrete footing with lots of rebar reinforcement for the boom's base. Triple trusses were installed in the attic above the boom, and metal strap was secured along the tops of ceiling joists (the bottom parts of trusses) to tie the entire roof structure together from corner to corner in a crisscross pattern.

Storing and accessing paint in a tidy manner can be a challenge to painters like Roy Dunn, owner of Auto Accents in Des Moines, Washington. In lieu of removing the top of every can of paint he must use to mix custom colors, Dunn simply screws an eyebolt into an edge of each can lid. This way, since he seldom needs more than a few drops at a time, he does not have to deal with paint residue on rims, or waste much material.

Tightly fastened eyebolts keep air and moisture out of cans as well as if they were sealed normally. This same philosophy could work for sealers and glues. Eyebolts or hook screws can be twisted into caps to make partial openings for controlled pouring. They make for leak-proof seals, provide immediate pouring outlets, and serve as a handy means for hanging tubes from pegboard or other hooks.

Overview

The means by which automotive workshops can be made more convenient and efficient are limited only by the imaginations of those who frequently work in them. Undoubtedly, you will soon come up with handy tips of your own as you work to outfit your shop in ways that suit your needs and preferences. When you come across a problem, spend time contemplating a viable and convenient solution. You might solve a number of step-saving problems with one simple idea.

No one has cornered the market on automotive workshops, as there are no designs that can perfectly meet everyone's needs or desires. Your shop should be personal. You must design, outfit, and decorate it the way you see fit. Should you come up with a maverick way of doing things that will save hours and hours of labor, share your idea with fellow auto enthusiasts by writing to automotive periodicals.

Mike Holiman installed a heavy-duty disc sander at the end of a workbench outfitted with a piece of steel plate for small welding jobs. The sander's motor rests below the workbench's surface, out of the way of other workbench activities. The sander's location is ideal for smoothing jagged edges on metal before and after welding.

Bill Snyder built his own stand for this buffing motor out of scrap metal he had on-hand. The old steel wheel makes a great base for the buffing motor. These kinds of inventive accessories save money and help to make workshops much more personal.

As important as shop design and outfitting may be to you, do not overlook safety concerns. The wide range of activities that take place in your shop will present conditions that can cause serious injuries to those who neglect to follow established and common sense safety procedures. Protective eye wear, hearing protection, gloves, respirators, and other appropriate personal safety items should be worn whenever you are involved with grinding, welding, metal cutting, painting, and other endeavors that present potential injury hazards. Keep these items stored next to specific work areas so they are immediately available at all times.

To your list of personal safety equipment add those accessories that make the entire working environment a safe place for users and visitors alike. Store soiled rags and shop towels in metal containers with lids to help prevent spontaneous combustion. Provide ample ventilation with heavy-duty fans at both ceiling and floor levels while involved with sanding, welding, grinding, painting, and other tasks that create polluted atmospheres. Erect portable barriers (saw horses) around pit openings, and be sure to immediately replace pit lids once a car has been moved.

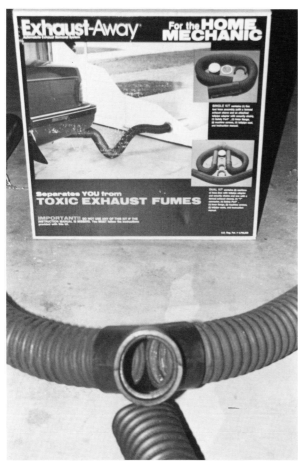

The Exhaust-Away automobile exhaust removal system is available in both single- and dual-exhaust models. This system was designed specifically for home use by the Crushproof Tubing Company and is based on their professional-use exhaust ventilation products. The crushproof flexible tubes can withstand temperatures up to 600° F, are 5ft long, and have a 3in diameter. For ease of storing, the single tube unscrews from the two-tube dual-exhaust model. An exclusive Safety Port fitting attaches to garage doors and has a hinged door which remains closed when not in use. The tailpipe adapter is a soft, gasket-like material that ensures a tight fit around tailpipes; a safety chain makes sure the tube does not come off until you are ready to take it off. Each kit comes with complete instructions and all of the hardware needed for its installation. Everyone who tunes engines in home garages and home-based automotive workshops should have an exhaust removal system.

The best way to store soiled shop towels is in a storage can designed specifically for that purpose. Certain oils saturated into shop towel material and smothered under the weight of several other towels can be subject to spontaneous combustion. To prevent this disaster, soiled rags and shop towels should be placed inside a metal container with a tight-fitting lid. Soiled shop towel cans feature a spring-loaded lid that is opened by a foot-operated lever. They are available at autobody paint and supply stores, hardware stores, and safety supply outlets.

Have extra sets of goggles, welding hoods, and respirators on hand for family members or visitors who stop by.

Be sure that all of the safety features on shop equipment are in proper operating condition. This includes such things as fusible links on parts-washing tub lids, shields on bench grinders, latches on flammable liquid storage cabinets, locking mechanisms on lifts and jack stands, and so on. Make certain that your first aid kit is clearly available and well stocked, too.

Safety must never take a back seat to any project undertaken in any shop. Always keep it at the front of your mind while planning for and then executing repair or maintenance procedures. Your workshop should be a place where you have fun, learn new techniques, and help others learn the ins and outs of auto care. You should expect to derive a great deal of pleasure from the convenience, accessibility, and other benefits of your special shop. This will all be greatly augmented by the inclusion of safety accessories followed by standard, recommended, and common sense practices.

It is hoped that the information in this book will help you design and outfit a shop that meets all of your needs, and that all of the activities conducted there prove to be safe and enjoyable.

An automotive workshop must always include a fully stocked first aid kit and at least two fire extinguishers in case one does not operate in an emergency. Complete first aid kits are available at safety and supply houses and at some hardware stores and lumber yards. Along with plenty of adhesive bandages, this kit should be equipped with eye-flushing utensils, large gauze bandages, tape, and rolls of gauze. Fire extinguishers are rated according to their ability to extinguish different kinds of fire. Class "A" is for normal combustibles like wood and paper; Class "B" is for flammable liquids; Class "C" is for fires involving electricity; and Class "D" is for metal fires, like aluminum or magnesium. The unit pictured is an "ABC" model, dry chemical extinguisher, good for normal combustibles, flammable liquids, and electrical fires. Plan to install at least two dry chemical extinguishers with ratings of at least a 2A, 10B, and C in your automotive workshop.

SOURCES

Listed below are the names, addresses, and telephone numbers of companies that participated in this book project by supplying information, photos, and/or samples of their construction or automotive tools and equipment. You are encouraged to call or write to these companies for more information about the products featured in this book, as well as for catalogs that include information about additional items they offer.

American Tool Companies, Inc.
P. O. Box 337
De Witt, NE 68341
(402) 683-2315

Autodesk Retail Products
11911 North Creek Parkway S.
Bothell, WA 98011
(800) 228-3601

Autotronic Controls Corporation
MSD Ignition
1490 Henry Brennan Drive
El Paso, TX 79936
(915) 855-7123

California Car Cover Company
15430 Cabrito Road
Van Nuys, CA 91406
(800) 423-5525

Campbell Hausfeld
100 Production Drive
Harrison, OH 45030
(513) 367-4811

The Chamberlain Group, Inc.
845 Larch Avenue
Elmhurst, IL 60126
(800) 528-9131

Cover-It Instant Garages
153 Main Street
P.O. Box 487
Ansonia, CT 06401
(800) 466-8600

Dremel
4915 21st Street
Racine, WI 53406-9989
(414) 554-1390

The Eastwood Company
580 Lancaster, Box 296
Malvern, PA 19355
(800) 345-1178

Exhaust-Away (Crush-Proof Tubing Co.)
P. O. Box 818
McComb, OH 45858
(800) 654-6858

Harbor Freight Tools
3491 Mission Oaks Blvd.
Camarillo, CA 93011
(800) 423-2567

Helsper Sewing Company
Sewn Products
36 Center Drive, Unit #3
Gilberts, IL 60136
(708) 428-5462

Hemmings Motor News
PO Box 100, Route 9W
Bennington, VT 05201
(802) 442-3101

HTP America, Inc.
261 Woodwork Lane
Palatine, IL 60067
(800) USA-WELD

Makita USA, Inc.
14930 Northam Street
La Mirada, CA 90638-5753
(714) 522-8088

Pine Ridge Enterprise
13165 Center Road
Bath, MI 48808
(517) 641-4881

Plano Molding Company
431 East South Street
Plano, IL 60545-0189
(708) 552-3111

PPG Industries, Inc.
19699 Progress Drive
Strongsville, OH 44136

Pro Motorcar Products
22025 U.S. Hwy. 19 North
Clearwater, FL 34625
(800) 323-1090

Sidewinder Products Corporation
320 Second Avenue North
Birmingham, AL 35204
(800) 999-3405

Simpson Strong Tie Company, Inc.
1470 Doolittle Drive
San Leandro, CA 94577
(800) 227-6342

Smithy Company
3023 East Second Street
The Dalles, OR 97058
(800) 345-6342

Snap-on Tools Corporation
2801 - 80th Street
Kenosha, WI 53141-1410
(800) 866-5748

The Stanley Works
1000 Stanley Drive
New Britain, CT 06050
(800) 551-5936

Sta-Put Color Pegs
23504 29th Avenue West
Lynnwood, WA 98036
(206) 483-9694

Vermont American
P. O. Box 340
Lincolnton, NC 28093-0340
(704) 735-7464

WESCO Autobody Supply
12532 NE 124th Street
Kirkland, WA 98033
(206) 823-5887

Wickliffe Industries, Inc.
P.O. Box 286
Wickliffe, OH 44092
(216) 256-1030

INDEX